MAYER SMITH

A Kingdom Built on Rain

Copyright © 2024 by Mayer Smith

All rights reserved. No part of this publication may be reproduced, stored or transmitted in any form or by any means, electronic, mechanical, photocopying, recording, scanning, or otherwise without written permission from the publisher. It is illegal to copy this book, post it to a website, or distribute it by any other means without permission.

This novel is entirely a work of fiction. The names, characters and incidents portrayed in it are the work of the author's imagination. Any resemblance to actual persons, living or dead, events or localities is entirely coincidental.

Mayer Smith asserts the moral right to be identified as the author of this work.

Mayer Smith has no responsibility for the persistence or accuracy of URLs for external or third-party Internet Websites referred to in this publication and does not guarantee that any content on such Websites is, or will remain, accurate or appropriate.

Designations used by companies to distinguish their products are often claimed as trademarks. All brand names and product names used in this book and on its cover are trade names, service marks, trademarks and registered trademarks of their respective owners. The publishers and the book are not associated with any product or vendor mentioned in this book. None of the companies referenced within the book have endorsed the book.

First edition

This book was professionally typeset on Reedsy.
Find out more at reedsy.com

Contents

1	The Arrival	1
2	The Portrait in the Attic	8
3	The Stranger in the Garden	14
4	Echoes in the Hallway	21
5	The Whispering Walls	28
6	Beneath the Surface	35
7	Echoes of the Past	42
8	The Awakening	48
9	Beneath the Surface	55
10	The Choice	62
11	The Breaking Point	69
12	The Heart of the Storm	76
13	The Shattered Veil	83
14	The Edge of Eternity	88
15	The Weight of Silence	95
16	The Heart of the Storm	102
17	The Breaking Point	108
18	The Reckoning	115
19	the Storm	122
20	The Threshold	129
21	The Shattering	136
22	The Final Choice	143
23	The Heart of the Storm	150
24	The Aftermath of Silence	157

25	Into the Abyss	165
26	The Last Whisper	172
27	The Storm's Return	179
28	The Weight of Silence	186
29	The Echo of Shadows	192
30	The Heart of the Storm	198
31	The Appraisal	204
32	A Flicker in the Dark	209
33	The Breaking Point	216

1

The Arrival

The rain came down in sheets, relentless and unforgiving, as if the heavens themselves had opened to mourn the loss of something precious. Elara Delcourt gripped the reins of her horse tightly, her fingers numb from the cold, as the wind howled through the vast, unyielding fields. The towering gates of Delcourt Manor loomed in the distance, a silhouette of gothic stone and ivy, half-swallowed by the mist. The manor, a relic of another age, stood as a symbol of her late husband's family's dwindling legacy, and now it would be her prison.

She had not wanted to come.

Her heart ached with the weight of her husband's untimely death, still so raw, still so sharp. But duty—ever the cruel companion of the grieving—demanded that she return. The inheritance. The legacy. And the endless eyes of society that expected her to uphold both. What else could she do? Elara had no family, no fortune of her own. She had been little more than a pawn in her husband's world, a world she now had to navigate alone.

The gates creaked open with a groan, as though the manor itself resented her arrival. She spurred her horse onward, the hooves striking against the rain-soaked earth, sending mud splattering behind her. Delcourt Manor, once a place of opulence, now felt like a tomb—a decaying testament to the power that had once flourished within its walls.

As she drew closer, the full scale of the house became apparent. Towering spires stretched into the heavy clouds, and the sprawling wings of the mansion were obscured by a thick veil of fog. The estate seemed to grow darker, more foreboding with each passing moment. Elara hesitated, staring up at the ivy-clad stone, her breath caught in her throat.

There it was, the heavy weight of the past pressing down on her. Her husband, Sebastian Delcourt, had died only two months ago, his death as sudden as it was mysterious. Rumors swirled like vultures, whispers of his illness, of his descent into madness, of the curse that plagued his family. His death had been a quiet affair, no great tragedy, no dramatic outpouring of grief. Just a closing of a door, an unremarkable end to a life filled with unspoken sorrows. But it was the things left behind, the inheritance, the manor—those were the real burdens she now carried.

Elara reined in her horse as they reached the front steps. A large oak door, stained dark with age, stood before her, guarded by two statues of stone lions. She dismounted carefully, her cloak swirling around her as she stepped forward. The heavy door swung open just before she could knock, revealing a servant who looked as though he had been expecting her all along.

"Lady Delcourt," the servant greeted her in a voice that was both polite and distant. "We have been awaiting your arrival."

His eyes were shadowed by the dim light, and he seemed uncomfortable in his own skin. His name, she knew, was Daniel. A man of few words, quiet and unobtrusive, much like the rest of the household staff. She had never learned much about him, nor had she cared to. But in that moment, she sensed something unsettling beneath his demeanor, something that made the hairs on the back of her neck stand on end.

"Thank you," Elara replied, her voice steady, though her heart raced. "I... I did not expect such a welcome." Her voice cracked slightly as she spoke, betraying the sorrow she had worked so hard to keep buried.

The servant nodded, stepping aside to allow her entry. As she crossed the threshold, the warmth of the fire in the grand hall hit her, though it did little to ease the chill in her bones. The manor was vast—far larger than she remembered, the high ceilings stretching upwards, decorated with ornate tapestries that seemed to watch her as she passed. The air inside felt thick, musty, as though the house had been holding its breath for years.

"The house is still as it was," Elara said quietly, though the words seemed to carry a weight far heavier than she intended. She had not visited the manor in over a year, not since Sebastian's illness had kept him away from his ancestral home. She had always found the place too oppressive, too full of memories that she wished to forget.

"Your rooms are prepared, Lady Delcourt," Daniel said, his voice offering no comfort. "Shall I show you to them?"

Elara nodded, feeling the weight of the words press into her chest. The cold, empty rooms were hers now. There was no escaping it, no escaping the life that had once been hers—now irrevocably changed by the loss of Sebastian.

As they walked through the house, the long corridors stretched before them like endless passageways into darkness. The only sound was the soft echo of their footsteps, a faint rustling of the heavy curtains as the wind outside howled against the stone walls. It was a place steeped in history, and yet, it felt like a place abandoned by time, forgotten by the world.

When they reached the staircase, Daniel paused. "Lady Delcourt," he said, his voice low, "there is something you should know." His eyes darted nervously to the side, as if he feared someone might be listening.

Elara stopped, turning to face him. "What is it?"

"There are rumors," he began, his words hesitant, as though he feared speaking them aloud. "About the manor. About the... Delcourt family."

Elara raised an eyebrow, curiosity mingling with suspicion.

"Rumors?"

He nodded, glancing down the hall as though he expected someone to appear at any moment. "Some say this house is cursed. That the rain brings death... and with it, madness."

Elara's heart skipped a beat. The rain. The endless rain that seemed to follow her wherever she went, as if it too was a part of the curse she had inherited by marrying Sebastian.

She forced a smile, though it felt hollow. "I'm sure it's nothing more than superstition."

Daniel said nothing, but his expression told her he didn't believe it. There was something in his eyes, something that made Elara uneasy. But she said nothing, merely nodded and continued up the stairs behind him.

Her room was at the end of a long, narrow hallway, and as she stepped inside, the familiar scent of old wood and dust hit her. The heavy curtains were drawn tight, blocking out any hint of the storm raging outside. The room was large, but it felt claustrophobic in its silence. The bed, draped in deep crimson velvet, looked untouched, as though no one had dared to enter for years.

Elara set her things down, her fingers trembling slightly as she unfastened her cloak. The fire crackled softly in the hearth, and for a moment, she allowed herself to breathe—deeply, steadily. She was here now, and there was no turning back.

As she glanced around the room, her eyes landed on the portrait above the mantel. It was of a woman, dark-eyed and fair, wearing the same rich crimson gown as the one draped across the bed. The resemblance was uncanny—so striking that Elara took an involuntary step closer.

The woman in the portrait had a haunting, sorrowful expression. Her lips, painted red, were slightly parted, as though she was about to speak. Her eyes, however, were what held Elara's gaze. There was something about them—something unnervingly familiar.

It was as if the woman in the portrait were watching her.

Before she could examine the painting further, a loud crack of thunder split the sky, shaking the walls of the manor. Elara's heart jumped in her chest, and she quickly turned away, her breath shallow. The storm had arrived in full force.

As she moved to the window to pull back the curtain, her reflection caught in the glass—pale and fragile, like the woman in the portrait. For a moment, she saw something flicker in the corner of the room, a shadow that seemed to move just out of the corner of her eye. Elara's pulse quickened, and she spun around, but the room was empty.

Only the rain outside. Only the house. Only the past.

And as the storm raged on, she realized that this house, these halls, would be her prison.

And somewhere, hidden in the dark recesses of Delcourt Manor, her husband's secrets waited—secrets that she was not yet ready to uncover.

2

The Portrait in the Attic

The storm hadn't relented. By the next morning, the skies were still shrouded in an impenetrable gray, and the rain beat against the windows of Delcourt Manor as though trying to claw its way inside. Elara sat by the fireplace in her bedroom, her hands wrapped around a steaming cup of tea. The fire provided little warmth against the oppressive chill that seemed to seep through the walls. It was the kind of cold that didn't just touch the skin but worked its way into the soul.

The portrait above the mantel loomed over her as she sipped her tea. Elara had spent much of the night tossing and turning, unable to shake the feeling that the woman in the painting was watching her. She had wanted to dismiss the thought as a trick of her imagination, a product of her grief and exhaustion. But now, in the daylight, the resemblance between herself and the painted figure was impossible to ignore.

The resemblance and the lingering unease it brought her were enough to draw her from her room. After dressing in a simple gown of deep blue wool, she ventured into the labyrinthine corridors of the manor. The air was heavy, carrying the faint scent of damp stone and old wood. Though the house was vast, her footsteps echoed as though it were empty, as though the walls themselves were listening.

It was Daniel who found her in the corridor, his quiet presence startling her out of her thoughts.

"Lady Delcourt," he said with a deferential bow. "Breakfast has been prepared in the dining room."

"I'm not hungry," Elara replied, her voice softer than she intended. She glanced toward the grand staircase. "But perhaps you could help me with something?"

"Of course." He straightened, though his expression remained wary. "What do you require?"

"Who is the woman in the portrait above the fireplace in my room?" she asked, studying his face for a reaction.

Daniel hesitated, his eyes flicking downward before meeting hers again. "That is Lady Marguerite Delcourt," he said carefully. "She was the wife of your husband's great-grandfather."

Elara waited for him to continue, but he didn't. "And?" she prompted.

"She... she met an unfortunate end," Daniel admitted reluctantly. "It's not a tale we speak of often."

"Why not?"

"It's said she died in sorrow," Daniel replied, his voice lowering. "Some believe her spirit lingers in the house, watching over it. Or haunting it, depending on who you ask."

Elara's stomach tightened. She had no patience for ghost stories, but there was something in Daniel's tone—an edge of fear—that made her chest ache with unease.

"Where can I learn more about her?" she asked. "Is there a library?"

"There is," Daniel said, his voice hesitant. "But if you're truly curious about Lady Marguerite, you might find answers in the attic. That's where many of the Delcourt family's belongings were stored after her death."

Elara nodded. "Thank you, Daniel. That will be all."

Though he bowed and left her without protest, she could feel the weight of his disapproval as she made her way toward the attic stairs. The upper levels of the manor were colder than the rest of the house, the stone walls damp and unwelcoming. The staircase that led to the attic was narrow and steep, the kind of place where one felt the need to glance over their shoulder with every step.

At the top, the door was stuck fast. Elara shoved it open with a grunt, and it creaked on its hinges, revealing a dark expanse of forgotten memories. The attic smelled of mildew and dust, the air so thick with it that she covered her mouth and nose with her handkerchief. Sunlight filtered through a small, dirty window, casting faint streaks of light across the cluttered space.

Furniture draped in white sheets stood like ghosts in the shadows. Stacks of crates and trunks lined the walls, each labeled in fading ink. She moved cautiously, her fingers trailing over the surfaces as she passed. The silence was almost oppressive, broken only by the occasional patter of rain on the roof.

Her eyes fell on a large, ornately carved trunk in the far corner. Something about it drew her closer, and when she reached it, she saw that the name "Marguerite Delcourt" was etched into the wood. Her pulse quickened as she knelt and lifted the heavy lid.

Inside were relics of another life: a collection of faded letters tied with a red ribbon, a silver comb adorned with pearls, a lace handkerchief embroidered with the initials "M.D." But what caught her attention was a small, water-stained portrait wrapped in delicate cloth. She pulled it out carefully and gasped.

It was a painting of Marguerite, smaller than the one in her room but no less striking. The resemblance was even more pronounced here, down to the curve of the lips and the tilt of the head. But what made her blood run cold was the expression. While the larger portrait had shown Marguerite with a melancholic air, this one portrayed something far darker—fear.

Her hands trembled as she studied the painting. The eyes seemed to bore into her, pleading, warning. The water damage had blurred the edges, creating the illusion that the figure was melting into the shadows. It was unnerving, and yet she couldn't look away.

"Elara."

The whisper was so faint she almost thought she imagined it. Her head whipped around, her heart pounding. "Who's there?"

Silence.

The shadows seemed to grow thicker, the corners of the attic darker than before. Elara's breath came faster as she stood, clutching the portrait to her chest. The air had changed, grown heavier, colder. She felt it then—a presence, as though someone were standing just behind her.

"Elara," the whisper came again, louder this time.

She spun around, but the attic was empty. Her knees threatened to give out beneath her as she stumbled toward the staircase. The painting still clutched in her hand, she descended as quickly as she could, the sensation of being watched pressing against her back with every step.

When she finally reached the lower floor, she leaned against the wall, struggling to steady her breathing. The house was silent, but it no longer felt still. It felt alive.

Elara's fingers tightened around the frame of the portrait. She stared at it again, her mind racing. Who had whispered her name? And why had the voice sounded so painfully familiar? She needed answers, but she wasn't sure she wanted them.

Her gaze drifted to the window at the end of the corridor. Outside, the rain continued to fall, relentless and unyielding, as though it would never stop.

3

The Stranger in the Garden

Elara stood in the drawing room, the heavy curtains drawn tightly against the gloom outside. The wind howled through the trees, sending branches scraping against the window as though trying to break through. She had tried to rest after the unsettling events in the attic, but sleep had eluded her. The image of the portrait—of Marguerite—kept swirling in her mind, and with it, the whisper that had called her name. It was a mystery she couldn't let go of, no matter how much she wanted to.

The manor was quiet, almost oppressively so. Since her arrival, only the steady presence of the staff had kept the house from feeling entirely abandoned, and yet something felt off. The silence between the walls seemed too thick, too suffocating. And then there was the constant, never-ending rain. It had been hours since the storm first broke, but the weather showed no signs of relenting. Elara felt as though the very earth itself was holding its breath, waiting for something to happen.

She wandered through the drawing room, her fingers trailing across the furniture, the old wood cold under her touch. A fire crackled softly in the hearth, but the warmth it offered did little to push back the chill in her bones. She needed to escape the suffocating atmosphere of the manor, even if only for a moment.

The large glass doors at the far end of the room beckoned her. The garden outside, though draped in mist and rain, was still a place of respite—a place where the stillness might offer her the clarity she so desperately needed. She wrapped her shawl tightly around her shoulders and stepped out into the rain, her boots sinking slightly into the damp earth as she made her way toward the wrought-iron gate that led to the gardens beyond.

The air was thick with moisture, the scent of wet earth and crushed leaves hanging in the air. The garden, once manicured and pristine, now lay overgrown and wild, the grass and vines reclaiming what had once been a place of beauty. The roses, long untended, hung in twisted, bedraggled clusters, their petals blackened by the storm. The trees loomed like dark sentinels, their branches reaching toward the sky as though trying to escape the oppressive atmosphere of the manor.

Elara walked deeper into the garden, her gaze scanning the shadows, the heavy rainfall blurring the world around her. She wanted to find peace, to escape the eerie quiet of the house, but the atmosphere only seemed to deepen the unease that had been growing in her chest. There was something about the garden—something hidden in its overgrown beauty—that set her nerves on edge.

As she rounded a corner, she froze.

A figure stood by the old stone fountain, a lone figure shrouded in a dark coat, their back turned to her. They were still, as though they, too, were waiting for something. For a moment, Elara thought she might be seeing things—perhaps it was the rain, the fog, or the late hour that made her vision hazy. But no, the figure was real.

Her heart skipped in her chest. Who was this person? The staff hadn't mentioned anyone else on the grounds. Elara instinctively took a step back, her breath quickening.

The figure turned slowly, as if sensing her presence, and Elara's breath caught in her throat.

It was a man. Tall, with dark hair and striking features, he looked as though he had stepped out of another time. His expression was unreadable, his eyes hidden in shadow beneath the brim of his hat. The rain ran off the edges of his coat, pooling around his feet, but he remained motionless, like a statue.

"Elara."

Her name came like a whisper on the wind, soft but clear.

Elara froze. The voice was deep, resonating, and somehow familiar, though she couldn't place where she had heard it before. Her pulse quickened, a sense of dread sweeping over her. She hadn't told anyone she was coming out to the garden, and the staff hadn't mentioned any visitors.

"Who are you?" she asked, her voice trembling more than she cared to admit.

The man didn't answer immediately. Instead, he took a step forward, his eyes locking onto hers. The intensity of his gaze made her feel exposed, as though he could see through her, past all her defenses. She took a cautious step back, her feet slipping slightly on the wet ground.

"Who are you?" she repeated, her voice firmer now, though doubt crept into her mind. Was he someone from the village? A traveler? She couldn't remember anyone who looked like him.

"I am Callum Wren," the man said, his voice low but smooth, like honey. "I've come to speak with you."

Elara's brow furrowed. The name was unfamiliar, but something about it made the hairs on the back of her neck stand on end. Callum Wren. The name sounded like a ghost of the past, a whisper in the wind that didn't belong in her present. He stepped closer, his eyes never leaving hers, and she instinctively took another step back, her heels sinking deeper into the mud.

"What do you want with me?" she demanded, though the words came out with less conviction than she had intended.

Callum didn't immediately respond. Instead, his gaze flickered to the overgrown roses, the darkened fountain, and the moss-covered statues that lined the garden. "This place holds many secrets," he said finally, his voice carrying a note of quiet sadness. "Some of them belong to you now."

Elara felt a chill run down her spine. His words hung in the air, heavy with meaning. She could feel the weight of them, the way they seemed to pull at something deep inside her, as though they were unearthing something long buried.

"I don't know what you mean," she said, trying to sound composed, but she couldn't help the flicker of fear that shone in her eyes. "How do you know my name? And what do you mean by secrets?"

He didn't answer immediately. Instead, his eyes shifted toward the manor, where the dark windows stared back at them, empty and watchful. There was a moment of silence before he spoke again.

"There are things in this house—things your husband never told you. Things about the family. The Delcourts have always had a... history. A history that doesn't stay buried for long."

Elara's heart raced. Her thoughts immediately turned to the journals she had found in the library—the ones her husband had kept hidden from her. Had he known something? Was Callum Wren talking about the same things she had uncovered?

"What are you saying?" she asked, her voice barely a whisper now. The air between them seemed to thicken, the storm still raging around them but distant, as though it were a mere backdrop to the conversation unfolding in the garden.

Callum stepped closer again, his presence imposing. His gaze was steady, unwavering, and there was an intensity to it that unsettled her. "I've been watching this house for a long time, Lady Delcourt. And I know what it's capable of."

Elara felt a tightness in her chest, her breath shallow as she struggled to keep her composure. The man's words didn't make sense—none of this did. Why was he here? What did he want from her?

"You're lying," she said, her voice trembling, though she fought to maintain control. "I don't know you. I don't know anything about what you're talking about."

"I think you do," Callum replied softly, his eyes narrowing slightly. "I think you know more than you realize."

Before Elara could respond, there was a sudden rustling behind them. Startled, she turned to see a figure emerging from the mist. It was Daniel, the servant who had shown her to her room when she first arrived.

"Lady Delcourt," he called out, his voice strained. "You must come inside. It's not safe to be out here in this storm."

Elara's gaze flickered back to Callum, but in that instant, he was gone. He had disappeared into the mist as though he had never been there at all.

Confused and unsettled, Elara turned back toward Daniel, but her mind was spinning with questions. Who was that man? And why had he spoken to her in such cryptic terms?

Daniel approached her, his eyes filled with concern. "Lady Delcourt, please. You shouldn't be out here. It's too dangerous."

Elara nodded absently, though her mind was elsewhere. The garden felt suddenly far colder, far emptier, and she couldn't shake the feeling that something—or someone—was watching her from the shadows.

The rain continued to fall. The storm wasn't over yet.

And somewhere, hidden within the dark corners of Delcourt Manor, more secrets waited.

4

Echoes in the Hallway

The following morning, Elara woke to the sound of the rain tapping against the windows, a persistent reminder of the storm that had gripped the land for days. The sky outside was still a blanket of heavy gray, casting the manor in a dull, oppressive light. The events of the previous night—her encounter with the mysterious stranger, Callum Wren, and the eerie feeling that had settled into her bones—loomed over her as she sat up in her bed, staring at the large, ornate clock on the wall that ticked away the passing minutes with a deliberate, unsettling slowness.

She had not been able to shake the feeling that something was wrong, something buried deep within the house. Every time she closed her eyes, she saw his face—Callum Wren's dark, intense eyes, the way he had spoken to her with such familiarity, as though they shared a history that she couldn't remember. His cryptic words echoed in her mind: "The Delcourts have always had a history. A history that doesn't stay buried for long."

Elara shook her head, trying to clear the thoughts. She could not afford to be consumed by paranoia. The manor was full of strange things, yes—but she had no reason to believe that a mysterious man lurking in the garden held any real threat. And yet, the warning in his eyes, the way he had disappeared without a trace, gnawed at her mind. What had he meant by the Delcourt family's history? Why had he come?

With a deep breath, she pushed the thoughts aside and dressed quickly, trying to focus on something other than the creeping dread in her chest. As she made her way down the grand staircase toward the dining room, she passed the hallway where the heavy, ornate portraits of her ancestors lined the walls—each face staring out from behind its gilded frame, their expressions frozen in time.

The house felt colder this morning, the air thick with silence. Every step Elara took echoed in the vastness of the manor, and the creaking of the floorboards beneath her feet seemed impossibly loud. The quiet was suffocating, and she could feel the weight of the house pressing in on her, as though it were alive, watching her every move.

When she entered the dining room, the atmosphere was no different. Daniel, as always, was waiting by the door to greet her, his expression serious but respectful.

"Lady Delcourt," he said with a bow. "Your breakfast is served."

Elara nodded, offering him a small smile. She was grateful for his quiet demeanor, for his ability to remain composed in the face of her mounting anxiety. But this morning, something in his eyes seemed... off. She couldn't place it, but there was a flicker of hesitation when he looked at her, almost as if he was debating whether to say something—something he wasn't sure he should.

"Is everything all right, Daniel?" she asked, her voice soft but insistent. "You seem... distant."

He hesitated before answering, his gaze darting toward the far end of the room where the large, unlit fireplace loomed, its empty hearth casting long shadows across the polished floor.

"I... I apologize, Lady Delcourt," he said, his voice tight. "It's nothing."

Elara watched him carefully. There was more to it than he was letting on, but she knew better than to press him further. Daniel was a man of few words, and any attempt to push him would likely only make him retreat further into his shell.

"I see," she said, forcing a smile. "Well, I'll be fine. Thank you."

As she took her seat at the long dining table, Elara's mind wandered again, returning to the mysterious stranger from the garden. Was it possible that she had imagined the entire encounter? The fog, the rain, the strange pull in her chest—it could have all been a figment of her imagination, a product of stress and sleepless nights. But that whisper, that deep voice calling her name—it felt too real. She couldn't ignore it.

"Lady Delcourt?" Daniel's voice broke through her thoughts.

She blinked, focusing on him once more. He was standing near the door, his hands clasped in front of him as though awaiting further instruction.

"There is a visitor," Daniel said, his tone betraying a hint of unease. "A gentleman. He's arrived on the estate, and he requests an audience with you."

Elara's heart skipped a beat. Another visitor? Could it be Callum? Was he somehow back? No, it didn't make sense. She hadn't told anyone about their encounter, and certainly no one outside the staff would know about it.

"Who is it?" she asked, keeping her voice steady.

"I... I'm not sure, my lady," Daniel said, his eyes flicking toward the door as though he, too, felt the weight of the unknown. "He refuses to give his name, only that he must speak with you. He's waiting outside, by the garden gate."

A cold shiver ran down Elara's spine. Her first instinct was to refuse the request, to send him away, but something in Daniel's expression—the unease, the discomfort—made her pause.

"Very well," she said, standing up. "I'll speak with him."

Daniel nodded and led her out of the dining room, through the hallways of the manor, and out toward the rear of the house where the garden gate stood. As they walked, Elara couldn't shake the feeling that the house was watching her, every creak of the floorboards, every shift in the air, echoing like a warning.

When they reached the gate, she saw him.

A man stood just outside the wrought-iron entrance, his dark coat clinging to him in the rain. He had his back to her, but there was no mistaking the silhouette—the broad shoulders, the long coat that swept behind him. The same stranger.

"Elara," the man said without turning, his voice like a low growl, but this time, there was no familiarity, no warmth in his tone. It was colder, more distant, as if the man before her was not the same one who had spoken to her in the garden the previous evening.

Her pulse quickened. She stood frozen for a moment, unsure of what to do. Callum Wren—or whoever this man was—had reappeared, and this time, there was something more dangerous in the air.

"Why are you here?" she asked, her voice shaking despite her best efforts. "What do you want from me?"

The man finally turned to face her, and Elara's breath caught in her throat. He was tall, with dark, intense eyes that seemed to pierce right through her. His face was sharp, angular, and his hair was disheveled, as if he had been traveling for some time. His expression was unreadable, but there was an undeniable tension in his posture, as though he were on the brink of something—something she didn't yet understand.

"I've come to warn you," the man said, his voice low but commanding. "You've awakened something in this house, something that should never have been disturbed."

A chill gripped Elara's heart. She glanced over her shoulder, almost expecting to see the manor itself looming behind her, its cold stone walls pressing in on her.

"What are you talking about?" she demanded. "What have I awakened?"

The man's gaze darkened, his jaw tightening. "The past, Lady Delcourt. The past never stays buried here. And neither do its secrets."

Before Elara could respond, the man stepped back, disappearing into the rain as quickly as he had appeared, leaving only the distant echo of his words to haunt her.

A storm had come. Not just outside—but inside the manor. The past was closing in, and Elara had no idea how to escape it.

As the garden gate swung back into place, Elara stood motionless, the weight of the man's warning sinking into her bones. Something was coming. Something terrible. And the house, as much as it had sheltered her, would not protect her from it.

The hallway seemed even darker as she made her way back inside, the shadows pressing closer, the quiet of the manor heavier. Each step felt like it might be her last, and yet, she couldn't stop moving forward.

The echoes were already in the hallway.

5

The Whispering Walls

Elara's hand trembled as she gripped the doorknob of her study, the cold brass sending a chill through her fingers. She had barely entered the house when the strange man, the one who had appeared so suddenly at the garden gate, vanished into the storm. His words still lingered in her mind, as though they had taken root in the very air she breathed. "You've awakened something in this house. Something that should never have been disturbed." The message had been cryptic, but it carried a weight of warning—of a danger lurking just beneath the surface of the manor she had come to call home.

But who was he? What did he mean by the past not staying buried?

With a determined breath, Elara pushed the door open and stepped into the study. The room was familiar, yet today it felt different—darker, as if the walls themselves had shifted since she'd last entered. The shelves of old books, the large desk by the window, the velvet chairs—everything seemed the same, and yet nothing felt right. It was as if the house were holding its breath, waiting for something to happen. She had to confront whatever was unraveling before her eyes, even if it meant facing what she feared the most: the truth.

The study, though often a refuge for her in times of uncertainty, now seemed to mock her. The very space that had once been her sanctuary now felt cold and unwelcoming. Elara walked toward the bookshelves, her footsteps barely making a sound against the thick rug beneath her feet. Her eyes scanned the rows of leather-bound books, most of which she had never dared to open. Her husband, Thomas, had kept this room locked more often than not, only allowing her to use it on rare occasions. He had claimed the study was for "business matters" only, never explaining the secrecy that surrounded it. She had never questioned him before, but now, with the strange events unfolding, she wondered if he had been hiding more than just his work.

Reaching for a volume near the edge of the shelf, Elara pulled it from its place. It was an old leather-bound book, its cover cracked with age. She didn't recognize the title, but it felt familiar in her hands, as though it had been waiting for her to touch it. A faint whisper echoed in her mind, and though it was only a fleeting sensation, Elara couldn't shake the feeling that this book had been placed here for a reason.

As she flipped the book open, a piece of yellowed parchment fell out, fluttering to the floor like a forgotten ghost. Elara bent down and picked it up carefully, her fingers brushing against the fragile paper. It was a letter, handwritten in delicate, flowing script. The words were faint, the ink faded by time, but she could still make out the first few lines.

To my dearest Marguerite,
   The time has come. The secret we buried so long ago must now be uncovered, or it will consume us all.

Elara's breath caught in her throat. The name Marguerite was the same as the woman in the portrait in the attic—the one whose eyes had haunted her dreams. The letter spoke of secrets, of something buried—something that could destroy them. The weight of the words pressed down on her, and for a moment, she felt dizzy, as though the very walls of the study were closing in around her. She had to know more.

Before she could read further, the sound of footsteps echoed from the hallway, pulling Elara out of her reverie. She quickly tucked the letter into the book and set it back on the shelf. A moment later, the door creaked open, and Daniel entered the room. His face was pale, his eyes shadowed with a mixture of concern and fear.

"Lady Delcourt," he said, his voice trembling ever so slightly. "There's something you need to see."

Elara frowned. "What is it, Daniel?"

Daniel glanced over his shoulder, as though ensuring no one was watching, before stepping closer. His voice dropped to a whisper. "There's been an incident in the cellar."

The word incident sent a chill down Elara's spine. The cellar, hidden beneath the manor, was a place she had never ventured. It was the one part of the house that had always felt off-limits, even to her husband. She had heard rumors among the staff, stories of strange occurrences and noises coming from beneath the floor, but she had never given them much thought. Now, though, those rumors seemed more like warnings.

"I don't understand," Elara said, her voice trembling. "What happened?"

"I'm not sure, my lady," Daniel replied. "But the door was left open—just a crack—and I heard something down there. Something moving. Something... unnatural."

Elara's heart raced. "Did you see anything?"

"No, my lady," Daniel said, his voice low. "But I heard... whispers."

Whispers. The word echoed in Elara's mind like a curse. She had heard whispers before—soft, unintelligible sounds that seemed to come from nowhere. But this was different. This was real. And it was coming from the cellar.

"Come with me," Daniel said urgently. "You need to see for yourself."

Elara hesitated. She knew she should be frightened, but something inside her compelled her to follow. Her curiosity, her need for answers, was stronger than her fear. The secrets of this house were starting to unravel, and she had to know what lay hidden in its depths.

She nodded, and without another word, Daniel led her out of the study and down the narrow hallway toward the stairs that led to the cellar. As they descended into the darkness, the air grew colder, the dampness of the stone walls pressing in on them. The faint sound of dripping water echoed from below, adding to the oppressive atmosphere.

At the bottom of the stairs, Daniel reached for a large, wrought-iron door that led into the cellar. It was ajar, just as he had said, and Elara could see nothing but blackness beyond. The light from the hallway barely reached the threshold, casting long shadows that seemed to stretch and writhe in the corners.

"Are you sure about this?" Elara asked, her voice tight with fear.

Daniel's face was pale, his lips pressed into a thin line. "I have to know, my lady."

He pushed the door open further, revealing the dim, flickering light of a lantern on a wooden crate. But it wasn't the lantern that drew Elara's attention. It was the marks. Strange, dark symbols had been scrawled along the walls, some of them smeared, as though hastily written with something—blood?—that had long since dried.

Elara's breath caught in her throat. She recognized the symbols. They were the same ones she had seen in the book she had found in the study, the same ones that had haunted her dreams. They were ancient, and they were a warning.

"What is this?" Elara whispered, her voice barely audible.

"I don't know," Daniel said, his voice trembling. "But I've seen them before. They're part of the old family curse."

Elara turned to him, her eyes wide with disbelief. "The curse? What are you talking about?"

Daniel swallowed hard, his eyes darting nervously to the symbols on the walls. "It's said that the Delcourt family is haunted by something—something dark and ancient. And those symbols… they're part of it."

Elara felt the room spin as the weight of his words settled in her chest. The Delcourt family curse. Was this what Callum Wren had been warning her about? Had the past, whatever it was, truly been buried so deep that no one had dared to uncover it? And now it was waking up.

As Elara stepped closer to the symbols, her foot brushed against something. She bent down and gasped as her fingers brushed against a cold, metal object half-buried in the dust. Pulling it out, she found a small, tarnished key. It was old—just like the house—and it seemed to hum with a strange energy, as though it had been waiting for her to find it.

"What is this?" Elara asked, holding the key up to the dim light.

Daniel's face went ashen. "That... that's the key to the locked room. The one no one's allowed to enter."

The locked room. Elara's heart skipped a beat. What could be inside that room? What had her family been hiding all these years?

She had to know.

Turning to Daniel, Elara made her decision. "We need to find the room. Now."

And with that, they both turned and ascended the stairs, the echoes of their footsteps following them into the unknown. The walls of Delcourt Manor were whispering, and Elara was beginning to understand that they had been waiting for her all along.

6

Beneath the Surface

The key felt cold and heavy in Elara's palm as she clutched it tightly, her heart racing in her chest. The dim lantern light flickered above her, casting strange, dancing shadows on the stone walls of the cellar. She could feel the weight of the moment pressing down on her, suffocating her with its silence. What was hidden behind the locked room? What secrets had been buried so long ago that her family had gone to such lengths to keep it sealed? She could sense that whatever lay ahead would change everything.

Elara's mind raced with questions as she climbed the narrow staircase back to the main floor. Daniel walked quietly beside her, his face pale, his gaze flickering nervously toward the walls as though expecting the house to reach out and swallow them whole. She could feel the same unease in the air, thick and oppressive, as if the house itself were alive and aware of their every movement.

"We need to find it," she said, her voice a mere whisper. "We need to unlock that room, Daniel."

He nodded but said nothing. His face was set in grim determination, but there was something in his eyes—something deep and haunted—that made Elara's stomach turn. He knew more than he was telling her. She could feel it, even if he wasn't willing to speak the truth aloud.

When they reached the main hallway, Elara turned toward the hidden passage that led to the west wing of the manor. She had never been down this way, not since she was a child. The old wooden doors at the end of the hall were almost always locked, their tarnished brass handles cold and unyielding. The memories of her childhood were clouded with a sense of unease whenever she thought about this part of the house. The west wing had always been shrouded in mystery, its rooms unused, its windows shuttered, its doors closed and bolted.

But now, with the key in her hand and the urge to uncover the truth driving her forward, she couldn't ignore it any longer.

"This way," she said, her voice steady despite the torrent of fear and confusion swirling within her.

They walked in silence, their footsteps muted by the thick rugs that covered the floor. The hallway was long and narrow, with portraits of long-forgotten ancestors lining the walls. The eyes of the painted figures seemed to follow her as she passed, their faces stern and unmoving. She couldn't help but feel that they were watching, judging, waiting for her to make a decision— waiting for her to open the door that had remained shut for so long.

When they reached the end of the hall, Elara stopped in front of the large wooden door. It stood like a sentinel, solid and unyielding. The tarnished brass handle gleamed faintly in the dim light of the hallway, almost beckoning her to take the next step. Her fingers hovered over the key, her breath shallow as her pulse quickened.

"Elara..." Daniel's voice was low, almost hesitant. "Are you sure you want to do this?"

She turned to him, her eyes hard with resolve. "We have no choice. Whatever is hidden in there, it's connected to all of this—the strange occurrences, the whispers, the warnings. It's all part of something much bigger than we understand. I need to know what my family has kept from me."

Daniel's face softened, a flicker of something like pity crossing his features, but he said nothing more. He didn't have to. She could see the fear in his eyes, the way he looked at the door as though it were a gate to hell. But Elara wasn't afraid anymore. At least, not of the truth.

She took a deep breath and inserted the key into the lock. It turned easily, with a soft click, and she pushed the door open.

The room beyond was small, its air thick with dust and the scent of decay. The walls were lined with shelves, each one stacked with old, yellowed books and odd artifacts that Elara didn't recognize. A large, ornate desk sat in the center of the room, its surface cluttered with papers, maps, and ancient-looking scrolls. But it wasn't the contents of the room that drew Elara's attention—it was the feeling. The suffocating, heavy feeling that seemed to pulse in the air, as though something malevolent had been waiting here for years.

Stepping inside, Elara's gaze fell upon a large, framed portrait hanging on the far wall. It depicted a woman with strikingly familiar features—a woman who looked almost identical to Elara herself. The same dark eyes, the same high cheekbones, the same raven-black hair. But there was something wrong about the painting. The woman in the portrait wore a twisted, almost manic smile, her eyes gleaming with an unsettling knowledge. Elara felt a shiver run down her spine.

"Who is she?" Elara asked, her voice barely above a whisper.

Daniel hesitated before answering, his eyes darting nervously to the floor. "That... that's Marguerite. The one the letter was addressed to."

Marguerite. Elara felt a cold weight settle over her. The name had been haunting her since she had discovered it in the letter earlier. It couldn't be a coincidence. Her family had been hiding something about this woman—about the past she had never been told.

She stepped closer to the portrait, her eyes locked on the twisted smile of the woman in the painting. It felt as if Marguerite were staring back at her, as though the painting was alive, watching, waiting for her to uncover the truth.

Suddenly, Elara's gaze shifted to the desk. A large, leather-bound journal sat open near the edge, its pages yellowed with age. The handwriting on the pages was faint but legible, and as Elara stepped closer, she could make out the words.

We have sealed the truth away for too long. The family must never know what happened in this house. The curse will consume us all if we do not keep it buried.

Her breath caught in her throat as she read the words, the weight of them settling in her chest like a leaden stone. Her family knew. They had known for generations, and they had done everything in their power to keep the truth from her. The curse, the darkness that had haunted the Delcourt bloodline—it was real. And it was waiting to consume her, just as it had consumed those who had come before her.

"Elara…" Daniel's voice broke through her thoughts, shaking her from her reverie. She turned to find him standing by the door, his face drawn and pale. "We shouldn't be here. We've already uncovered too much."

Elara's gaze flickered to him, and for a moment, she saw something in his eyes—something dark and desperate. Was he hiding something? Was he part of this secret, too? Had he known all along?

"No," she said, her voice hardening with resolve. "We're not leaving until we know everything."

She turned back to the journal, flipping through the pages with trembling hands. As she read, the horrifying truth became clearer. The Delcourt family had made a pact long ago—a pact to keep an ancient power sealed within the walls of the manor. But over the years, the seal had weakened, and now, the darkness was beginning to stir once again. It was no coincidence that she had come into this house—it was her bloodline, her connection to the past that had triggered the awakening of something malevolent.

The more Elara read, the clearer it became. Her ancestors had not only hidden the truth from her—they had actively protected her from it, even if it meant keeping her in the dark about the legacy she had inherited. The whispers, the strange occurrences in the manor—they were signs that the curse was unraveling.

"Elara..." Daniel's voice was strained now, his voice barely a whisper. "We can't stop it. It's too late."

She looked up from the journal, her heart hammering in her chest. The room had grown colder, the shadows deeper, as though the very walls were closing in on her. And then she heard it—the soft, low whisper of a voice, coming from somewhere behind her. It was faint at first, indistinct, like a murmur carried on the wind.

"Elara..."

Her name. A low, haunting call, as though the house itself were reaching out to her.

"Elara..." the voice called again, closer this time, more insistent.

She spun around, but there was nothing there. The room was empty, the air still.

"Elara, we've been waiting for you..."

The voice was familiar, but she couldn't place it. It was a voice from the past—someone she should have known, someone she had forgotten.

The whispers grew louder, surrounding her, pressing in from every corner of the room. Elara's breath quickened as the walls seemed to close in on her. The shadows lengthened, reaching out toward her like hands of darkness. And then, before she could react, the room plunged into darkness, the lantern flickering out with a sharp hiss.

The darkness swallowed her whole.

7

Echoes of the Past

The darkness swallowed Elara whole, its thick, oppressive weight pressing in on her chest, suffocating her. She could no longer hear the whispering voice that had surrounded her moments before, but the cold, malevolent presence lingered, heavy in the air. Her heart hammered in her chest as she stood frozen in the pitch-black room, the oppressive silence stretching on for what felt like an eternity.

"Elara?" Daniel's voice broke through the stillness, trembling, barely audible.

She reached out, her hand brushing against the desk. Her fingers trailed along the edge, searching for something—anything—familiar, anything that could ground her in this nightmare. Her breathing was shallow, her every instinct screaming at her to run, but her feet felt like lead. Her body refused to move, as though it were caught in the grip of something far more powerful than her own will.

"Elara!" Daniel's voice broke again, louder this time, closer. She could hear the panic in his tone, and a flicker of awareness stirred within her.

"Daniel," she whispered hoarsely, her voice thick with fear. She reached out blindly, feeling the coolness of the air around her, searching for the source of his voice.

A sudden flicker of light pierced the darkness, and the room was momentarily illuminated by a soft, golden glow. Elara squinted, trying to focus, and saw Daniel standing a few feet away, holding a lantern in his trembling hands. His face was pale, his eyes wide with fear.

"Elara," he said again, his voice barely above a whisper. "We have to get out of here. Now."

She looked at him, her body frozen in place. "What... what happened?" she asked, her voice hoarse.

"I don't know," he replied, stepping closer to her. "But it's not safe here. The house—it's changing. Something is waking up."

Elara swallowed hard, her throat tight. The words in the journal had warned her of something like this—something dark and ancient stirring within the walls of the manor. But hearing Daniel speak of it, seeing the fear in his eyes, made it feel all too real. She knew that she had to face whatever was coming, but a part of her was terrified that it was already too late.

"We need to find out what's going on," she said, her voice gaining strength despite the terror that gnawed at her. "I need to know what my family is hiding. I need to know what I'm a part of."

Daniel hesitated, his gaze flickering toward the door, then back to Elara. "I don't think you're ready for this," he said, his voice strained. "You don't understand what we're dealing with. The Delcourt family—they made a deal with something ancient. Something that shouldn't be disturbed."

Elara's pulse quickened as his words echoed in her mind. The curse. The darkness that had haunted the Delcourt bloodline for generations. She had always believed the stories were mere myths, but now, in the face of the overwhelming fear in Daniel's eyes, she could no longer deny the truth. This wasn't a simple family secret—it was something far darker, far more dangerous.

"Elara," Daniel said, his voice low and desperate, "We have to leave. You don't know what you're dealing with. You don't know what this house can do."

Her chest tightened as she looked at him, the flickering light of the lantern casting his face in sharp relief. For the first time, she saw the depth of his fear. There was something in his eyes— a recognition, a sorrow—that unsettled her. Something in him knew more than he was willing to share, and it made Elara's gut twist with suspicion.

"No," she said, her voice firm despite the growing sense of

dread. "I can't leave. Not yet."

She turned away from him and moved toward the desk, her eyes scanning the scattered papers. The journal still lay open, its pages curling at the edges from age. The symbols she had seen earlier seemed to glow faintly in the dim light, as though they were alive, watching her. She could feel them calling to her, beckoning her to understand—to see the truth that had been hidden from her for so long.

"Elara, please," Daniel said, his voice breaking. "This is not just about the house. It's about you. The Delcourt bloodline—it's cursed. There's no escaping it."

She looked up at him, her expression hardening. "I don't care about curses," she said, her voice icy. "I care about the truth. The truth about my family. The truth about what's happening to me."

Daniel took a step toward her, his hand reaching out as though to stop her, but he hesitated. He looked torn, conflicted, as though he was struggling with something deep inside him.

"I can't let you do this," he whispered, his voice filled with sorrow. "You don't understand what will happen if you keep going. The past—it's already caught up with you."

Elara's eyes narrowed as she turned back to the journal, her fingers skimming the pages. The words, faint but still legible, spoke of a time long ago—a time when her ancestors had made a dark pact, sealing away an ancient power to protect the family line. But that power, it seemed, was never truly gone. It was still there, lurking in the shadows of the manor, waiting for the right moment to break free.

"Elara…" Daniel's voice trembled again. "Please. Let it go. There's nothing more you can do."

She looked up at him, her expression softening for just a moment. "I have to know," she said, her voice steady. "I need to understand what's been hidden from me."

As she spoke the words, a cold gust of wind suddenly swept through the room, extinguishing the lantern in Daniel's hand. The light disappeared, plunging them both back into darkness. The temperature in the room dropped sharply, and Elara felt a chill crawl down her spine. The air seemed to hum with a strange energy, and the walls, which had once felt solid and secure, now seemed to pulse with an almost sentient awareness.

"Get away from the desk," Daniel warned, his voice frantic.

But it was too late. The moment Elara's fingers brushed the edges of the journal, the room seemed to shift. The shadows lengthened, twisting and curling as though they were alive. The faintest whispering began again, low and insistent, rising from the corners of the room like the sound of a thousand voices speaking in unison.

"Elara," Daniel hissed, grabbing her arm, pulling her back. "We have to leave now! It's happening!"

But Elara could barely hear him over the rising cacophony. The whispers grew louder, closer, their voices intertwining with her own thoughts, as though they were trying to drown her in their insidious murmurings. Her head spun, and for a moment, she could no longer tell where the room ended and the darkness began. It was as if she were falling into the very walls of the manor, sinking deeper and deeper into the past.

"Listen to me, Elara," Daniel pleaded, his grip tightening on her arm. "You're awakening something—something that was never meant to be unleashed. You don't understand what you've done."

Suddenly, the whispers stopped. Silence fell, thick and suffocating. Elara's heart pounded in her chest as she looked around, her eyes wide, her breath shallow. She could still feel the presence in the room—the weight of something ancient and powerful that was watching her, waiting.

And then, in the silence, she heard a voice.

A voice she recognized.

"Elara..."

Her breath caught in her throat, and she spun toward the sound, her eyes wide with disbelief.

It was a voice she had heard before. In the portrait. In the letter.

It was Marguerite.

8

The Awakening

The voice echoed through the suffocating silence, soft but unmistakable, as if it were coming from somewhere deep within the walls. Elara's pulse quickened, her fingers trembling as she clutched the desk for support. The shadows in the room seemed to stretch further, curling and twisting around her, pressing in on her from every side. For a moment, she couldn't breathe, as if the very air had turned to liquid, thick and oppressive.

"Elara..." The voice called her name again, lingering in the space between reality and madness. It was low, melodic, but there was an undeniable edge to it. A whisper carried on the wind, yet it felt as if it were coming from somewhere much closer. From somewhere within her.

"Elara, you've finally come."

Her breath caught in her throat as the words sank in, and she knew, without a doubt, that the voice belonged to Marguerite.

The woman in the portrait. The woman who had haunted her thoughts ever since she first laid eyes on that twisted, smiling face. The woman who had been the key to this entire house of secrets.

"Elara..." Daniel's voice broke through the tension, his grip tightening on her arm. "We need to get out of here. Now."

She turned to him, her eyes wide with fear. He looked panicked, his face pale, his eyes darting nervously toward the door. There was something in his expression—something that hinted at a deep, underlying fear. But there was no time to address it. Elara's gaze shifted back to the darkening room, her mind whirling with questions, with suspicions.

"I... I heard her," Elara whispered, her voice shaking. "Marguerite... she's here."

Daniel's face twisted with fear, his hand clenching around hers as though to anchor her. "No," he breathed, shaking his head. "This isn't her. This isn't her anymore."

Before Elara could respond, the shadows in the room shifted again, coiling and expanding, as though the very fabric of the space itself were beginning to unravel. The air grew colder, and an unnatural hum filled the room, vibrating through her bones. Her eyes darted to the walls, the corners of the room, her heart racing in her chest.

"Elara..." The voice echoed once more, louder this time, tinged with an almost pleading quality. "You must understand. The time has come."

She looked around, trying to locate the source of the voice, but it was as if the walls themselves were speaking to her. "What do you want from me?" she shouted into the darkness, her voice trembling with a mixture of defiance and fear. "What is this place? What is happening?"

A slow, almost mournful laugh rippled through the room, and the temperature dropped even further. Elara shivered violently, her teeth chattering. The shadows seemed to grow more solid, as though they were beginning to take form. The corners of the room, once shrouded in darkness, now pulsed with an eerie glow, revealing the outline of something—or someone—just beyond her reach.

"Don't be afraid, Elara," the voice cooed, now unmistakably coming from within the shadows. "I've been waiting for you. Waiting for you to unlock what was always meant to be yours."

Elara's breath caught in her throat. She stumbled backward, her heart pounding in her chest. This was too much. She had crossed a line, and now there was no turning back. The room was alive, and whatever Marguerite had become—it wasn't human anymore.

"Elara, we need to leave. Now." Daniel's voice broke through the mounting tension, but it was strained, fearful.

But Elara couldn't move. Her eyes locked onto the center of the room, where the shadows seemed to pool and congeal. A figure slowly materialized, shrouded in a cloak of darkness, her features indistinct at first, but gradually taking shape.

"Elara…" the figure murmured, her voice both distant and near, as though she were speaking from the very marrow of Elara's bones. "It's all been set in motion."

The figure stepped forward, revealing the face of Marguerite. Her eyes gleamed with an unnatural light, her smile twisted and cruel. Her skin seemed to shimmer, almost translucent, as though she were made of something otherworldly. Her presence filled the room, and Elara felt her heart skip a beat. This was no longer just a painting. No longer just a memory. The woman in front of her was something entirely different—something ancient and powerful.

"I don't understand…" Elara whispered, her voice cracking with the weight of her words.

Marguerite's lips curled into a smile, but there was no warmth in it. "Of course you don't," she said, her voice laced with an eerie sweetness. "But you will. Soon."

The figure stepped closer, and Elara felt an icy chill rush over her. It was as though the air had become thick with frost, each breath she took stabbing into her lungs. Her entire body felt as though it were being pulled toward the figure, as though some unseen force were drawing her in.

"Elara," Daniel said urgently, his voice breaking as he tried to pull her away. But his grip on her arm was weak, as though his strength was draining away. She looked back at him, confusion clouding her mind.

"What's happening to you?" she whispered, her voice hoarse.

But Daniel didn't answer. His face was pale, his features drawn tight in a grimace of pain. His body shook violently, his hands trembling as though he were trying to fight against something, but failing.

The shadows around Marguerite deepened, swirling like an ocean storm. The figure's eyes glowed brighter now, the unnatural light spilling out like a beacon, illuminating the room with an eerie, cold glow.

"Elara," Marguerite purred, her voice dripping with malevolence. "You don't realize the power you've awakened. This house—this place—is more than just a home. It is the cradle of what was meant to be."

Elara's breath hitched in her chest. She felt the ground beneath her feet tremble, the walls shifting as though they were alive. She could hear the whispers again, rising around her like a chorus of voices, each one calling her name, urging her to come closer.

"No..." Elara gasped, shaking her head. "I won't do this. I won't let you control me."

But Marguerite's laugh echoed through the room, chilling her to the bone. "Control?" she said, her voice dripping with dark amusement. "You were never in control, Elara. It was always meant to be this way. The bloodline runs through your veins. You are the one we've been waiting for."

Elara staggered backward, her mind racing, her pulse pounding in her ears. Her body felt heavy, as though the very air was pressing in on her, suffocating her. The weight of the truth was too much to bear. This was the curse. The dark power her family had kept hidden for generations. It was not just a story—it was real.

"You've been chosen," Marguerite continued, her voice growing stronger, more commanding. "This is your birthright. The darkness, the power, it has always been yours to claim. You will bring forth the reign of the Delcourt family. The kingdom we have longed for."

"No..." Elara whispered again, her voice barely audible. "I won't..."

But Marguerite's smile only grew wider, her eyes gleaming with an unsettling joy. "You have no choice. It's in your blood. You cannot fight it."

Elara felt her knees buckle beneath her, the weight of the truth crashing down on her. The room spun, and she reached out, grabbing hold of the desk to steady herself. The shadows around Marguerite twisted and coiled, wrapping themselves around her like a cloak.

"Elara, please," Daniel whispered, his voice strained. "Don't listen to her."

But Elara could no longer hear him. Her mind was drowning in the weight of the revelation, the truth she had never wanted to accept but had now been forced to confront.

The whispers rose again, louder and more insistent, filling her mind with their relentless voices.

"Elara..."

"Elara..."

Her name was the only thing she could hear. The darkness swirled around her, consuming everything else, until all that remained was Marguerite's face, glowing with an unearthly light.

"Elara," Marguerite said one final time, her voice softer now, almost tender. "You've come home."

And then the room went dark.

9

Beneath the Surface

Elara's eyes fluttered open, but the world around her was no longer the same. The air was thick with the scent of damp earth, cool and heavy, and the ground beneath her was uneven, slick with moisture. She could hear the faintest sound of water dripping somewhere in the distance. Her body ached, as though she had been bruised in every part. Her head throbbed with a dull, relentless pain, and her thoughts were sluggish, tangled in confusion.

She tried to move, but the air seemed to press down on her, as though she were trapped beneath the weight of a thousand years. Slowly, she pushed herself to a sitting position, her hands trembling as they pressed against the cold stone beneath her. Her heart raced, but the suffocating darkness around her made it impossible to see.

"Elara…"

The voice—a soft whisper—floated through the oppressive air.

It was familiar, yet distant. It was as though it were calling to her from far away, through a veil of shadows and secrets.

"Elara..." the voice repeated, this time closer, unmistakably real.

Her breath caught in her throat as she recognized the voice. It was Daniel. She tried to speak, but her throat was dry, as though she hadn't spoken in days. She opened her mouth, forcing a sound out, but it came out as a hoarse croak.

"Daniel?" she rasped, her voice cracking. But there was no reply. She scrambled to her feet, feeling the stone walls of the space around her, the jagged edges scraping against her skin. She had to find him. She had to get out of this place.

The air was damp and cold, seeping into her bones, but there was something else—something darker—that she could feel in the pit of her stomach. The heavy, ominous presence from before hadn't left. It was as though it were lurking, waiting for her to make the wrong move. Elara's hands fumbled over the surface of the walls, searching for a door, a window—anything that could lead her back to reality. The room was empty. No furniture. No signs of life. Just cold stone and the endless hum of silence.

"Elara..." the voice called again, this time almost directly in front of her.

She froze, her heart hammering in her chest. Her eyes were wide, her pulse racing. She could feel it now—a presence standing in the dark, just beyond her reach. She strained her eyes, but there was nothing. No outline. No figure.

"Elara, don't be afraid."

She blinked, and for a split second, she thought she saw something—a silhouette—just beyond the reach of the faint light filtering through cracks in the stone. But when she blinked again, it was gone. The shadows remained, stretching across the room like dark tendrils, clinging to the walls and ceiling.

Her hands were clammy as she pressed them against the stone, trying to steady herself. Her mind raced, trying to piece together what had happened, but the memories were slipping away, like smoke in the wind. The last thing she could remember clearly was the figure of Marguerite—her face twisted, her eyes glowing with that unnatural light. And then... everything had gone black.

"Elara."

This time, the voice was unmistakable. It wasn't just in her mind. It was real. Right in front of her. She swallowed hard and took a step forward, her heart in her throat.

"Daniel?" she called again, this time more forcefully.

The darkness seemed to shift. The shadows that had once seemed like solid, impenetrable walls began to move, curling away from the walls as though they were retreating. A faint light flickered ahead, and as Elara stepped closer, the room began to take shape. She blinked, her eyes straining against the sudden change.

The walls were covered in damp moss, and the floor beneath her was a mixture of stone and mud. Water trickled down the sides of the walls, the sound echoing in the silence. Her breath fogged in front of her, and her skin prickled with the cold. As she took another step forward, she stumbled over something—something soft, a fabric, a cloak, lying on the ground.

Her heart skipped a beat, and she quickly knelt beside it. The fabric was torn and stained with something dark—blood. Elara's fingers trembled as she lifted it, but before she could fully take in what it was, a voice cut through the stillness again. It was Daniel's voice, but this time it wasn't calling her name. It was different. The tone was strained, desperate.

"Elara, no!" he shouted.

She whipped around, her breath caught in her throat. His voice echoed from deeper within the darkness, but there was something off about it. It wasn't just panic—it was fear, raw and primal. The kind of fear that could only be born from knowing something terrible was about to happen.

"Daniel!" Elara shouted, her voice breaking. "Where are you? What's going on?"

But the only response was the sound of rushing water. The cold, eerie rush of water, so loud it drowned out everything else. Her heart raced as she turned in the direction of the sound, her feet slipping on the wet floor. She moved faster, her breath coming in ragged gasps, the shadows closing in around her.

The further she moved, the stronger the presence became. It wrapped itself around her, coiling tighter and tighter with each step. She could feel it, pressing against her chest, forcing the air from her lungs. The walls seemed to narrow, the shadows seemed to grow darker, more oppressive.

"Elara..." The voice came again, this time softer, almost soothing.

She froze, her skin prickling. She knew that voice.

It was Marguerite.

But it wasn't just her voice. There was something else layered beneath it. A darkness, an energy that seeped into her very bones.

"Elara..." The whisper wrapped itself around her, seeping into her mind, coaxing her forward. "Come closer."

Elara stepped back, shaking her head. No. She couldn't. She had to find Daniel. She had to get out of this nightmare. She had to...

The ground beneath her suddenly shifted, and she stumbled, her hands reaching out for support. The stone walls closed in around her, and the air grew impossibly thick. The shadows stretched, reaching for her, and she could hear them now—

the whispers—rising, louder, all around her, as if they were speaking in unison. Their voices were so close, so insistent, and for a moment, Elara couldn't tell if they were real or if they were just in her mind.

"Elara…" The whisper was louder now, directly in her ear. "You cannot escape."

Her breath caught in her throat. It wasn't just the house. It was the curse. The dark presence that had been waiting for her all this time, that had been calling to her, that had always known her name.

"Elara, come home."

Her feet moved before she could stop them, her body moving on its own accord, drawn by the pull of the darkness, pulled toward the voice. The room spun around her, and for a moment, she felt dizzy, as though she were no longer in control of her own body. The ground beneath her feet seemed to shift, the stone turning into something softer, something more alive. The whispers grew louder, their voices filling her ears, drowning out everything else.

"Elara…" Marguerite's voice was no longer a whisper. It was a command. "Come to me."

She stumbled forward, and then, out of the corner of her eye, she saw a figure moving toward her—tall, shadowed, and familiar. Her heart stopped.

"Daniel?" she whispered, but the figure didn't answer. It only continued to approach, its silhouette becoming clearer, darker. As the figure drew closer, Elara's breath hitched. It was Daniel—but it wasn't. His eyes glowed with that same unnatural light, his face twisted in a grimace.

"Elara," he whispered, his voice cracked. "You should have listened."

She tried to speak, but the words wouldn't come. The shadows around her grew thick, wrapping themselves around her like chains, pulling her toward the figure, toward the darkness. It was too much. She couldn't breathe. She couldn't think. She was falling.

Falling into the abyss.

10

The Choice

The room was no longer silent.

Elara's heart pounded in her chest, each beat a drum, each breath a gasp of panic. The air was thick with the scent of damp earth, and her body felt heavy as if gravity itself had turned against her. Shadows loomed on every side, clinging to the walls like old memories, suffocating, and endless. The presence she had felt earlier, like an oppressive weight pressing on her chest, was now everywhere—close, so close, she could almost taste it.

She could feel her pulse thrumming in her throat, a cold sweat dampening her brow. She tried to move, but her legs were frozen, trapped in the deepening darkness that coiled around her like a living thing. The figure standing in front of her—Daniel—seemed to shimmer and flicker in the dim light, his form wavering like a mirage.

"Daniel?" Elara whispered, her voice trembling. The words felt weak, but they were the only thing she could muster. "What's happening? Please... what's going on?"

But Daniel—no, the thing that had once been Daniel—didn't answer. His eyes glowed, unnatural, reflecting something she couldn't place. Something dark and ancient. His face was twisted, his mouth pulled into a grimace that was half pain, half something else—something malevolent.

"Daniel," she said again, louder now, reaching for him, her hand trembling. "Where are you? What's happened to you?"

For a moment, the flickering form of the figure seemed to hesitate, as if unsure of its next move. But then, just as quickly, the air around her grew colder, and a laugh—low, mocking, and familiar—sounded from the shadows. It came from somewhere else, somewhere deep, but it resonated within her, twisting something in her gut.

Marguerite's laughter.

"Elara..." The voice, this time, was not from Daniel, but from the darkness itself. It slid into her mind, filling her thoughts with the weight of an ancient presence. "You are so naive."

The shadows around her rippled, shifting like dark water, and suddenly, she felt as though she were being drawn into them, swallowed whole. Panic surged through her, and she fought against it, pushing back, forcing herself to focus. Her fingers brushed against something cold, and she snapped her head around to see that the walls of the chamber were no longer stone. The walls had transformed into something else—something living, something breathing.

The walls were made of roots.

Roots that curled upward, winding their way around the room, their tendrils thick and suffocating. Elara's breath caught in her throat as she looked up and saw the ceiling—no longer a ceiling, but a mass of tangled vines that seemed to pulse with a dark energy. The air, heavy with the scent of moss and decay, felt as though it was closing in on her, thick and impenetrable.

"Elara," Marguerite's voice whispered again, now directly in her ear. She spun around, her eyes wild, but there was no one there. "You can't escape what you've awakened."

The shadows closed in around her like a shroud, darkening her vision, making it impossible to see clearly. Her thoughts raced, her heart pounding. What was happening? What was this place? The truth—the horrible truth—began to settle in her bones. She had always known there was something more to this house, something more to the story of her family's legacy. But this—this was something else entirely.

"Elara…"

She turned, heart leaping in her chest, her breath catching. There, at the far end of the room, the figure of Daniel was moving toward her, his eyes glowing with that eerie light. He reached out a hand toward her, but it wasn't the Daniel she knew. This figure—this thing—was a reflection of him, an echo of the person she had once loved.

"Elara…" The voice that came from him now was low, strained, barely recognizable. "Come with me. I can help you."

Elara shook her head violently, backing away. "No," she whispered, her voice breaking. "No, I can't. You're not Daniel. You're not him."

The thing—Daniel's doppelganger—stopped, its gaze fixed on her with an intensity that felt like it could burn right through her. Its mouth twisted into a cruel smile, and for a moment, Elara could see something flicker behind its eyes—something darker than she could ever have imagined. Something ancient and powerful.

"You never understood, did you?" the thing that was Daniel whispered, stepping closer. "You never understood why you were chosen."

Elara's mind reeled, struggling to grasp the meaning behind the words. Chosen? Chosen for what? And why did it feel like everything was happening too fast, like she was trapped in a nightmare that had no escape?

"I was chosen," the thing continued, its voice like ice scraping against her skin. "Just as you were, Elara. We were always meant to find each other."

"No," Elara gasped, shaking her head. "You're wrong. This… this isn't right. You're not him!"

But the figure—Daniel's twisted reflection—took another step toward her, his eyes gleaming in the darkness. The shadows that had once been mere wisps were now alive, swirling around him like a cloak, and with every step, the room seemed to warp, the roots and vines pulsing with a malevolent energy. The floor beneath Elara's feet began to tremble, and she could hear a low hum, a vibration, that seemed to emanate from the walls themselves.

"Elara..." the figure said again, his voice more insistent now. "Don't fight it. We are one. You belong here."

"No," Elara gasped, stumbling backward. Her eyes darted around the room, desperately searching for some way out. But there was nothing. No escape. The walls, the floor, the vines—they were all closing in on her. There was nowhere left to run.

The presence of Marguerite loomed over her, like a dark cloud, suffocating, oppressive. And then, for a moment, the vines parted, revealing something in the center of the room—a pool of water. Black water, swirling and shimmering with an eerie light. It was as though it were alive, its surface rippling with the reflections of a thousand distant stars.

"Elara," the voice called again. This time, it was Marguerite's voice. "Come to me."

The pool beckoned. It called to her with a force she couldn't explain. And, despite every instinct screaming at her to turn away, she felt her feet moving toward it. The room seemed to spin, the walls closing in, the shadows whispering in her ears.

"You must choose," the figure that was Daniel said, his voice now hollow, distant. "Choose the path of the Delcourt bloodline. Join us, Elara. Or…"

He let the words hang in the air, heavy with unspoken meaning. And that was when Elara felt it—the weight of the decision bearing down on her.

Her mind was a blur of fear, confusion, and desperation. The water called to her, its surface reflecting the darkness that now consumed the room. And somewhere in the distance, she could hear the faintest sound—the sound of a heart beating, a heart she recognized.

Daniel. The real Daniel. But he was so far away, locked in the grip of whatever dark power this place had over him. And yet… she could feel him, could hear his voice calling to her through the dark, telling her to fight, to resist, to hold on to who she was.

The figure of Daniel—the twisted shadow—reached out, and Elara felt herself drawn forward, her body moving against her will.

"You must choose, Elara. Join us, or be lost forever."

The water shimmered in front of her, the reflection growing clearer. And for a moment, she saw something—a glimpse of herself. But it wasn't the Elara she knew. It was someone else—someone standing at the edge of a precipice, staring into the abyss, her heart torn between two worlds.

The choice was before her.

But would she take it?

11

The Breaking Point

Elara's pulse thrummed in her ears, each beat a hammer striking against her chest. Her legs were numb, her mind a swirl of confusion, but one thing was clear—she couldn't stay in this place any longer. The figure of Daniel, the twisted reflection of the man she had once known, stood before her, his eyes glowing with an unnatural light. The darkness seemed to crawl across the room, the air thick with an oppressive force that clawed at her from every direction.

"You must choose," the figure of Daniel said again, his voice no longer familiar. It was cold, detached, like a shadow of the man she had loved. "Join us, Elara. You were born for this. You belong with us."

Elara's body shook as she took a step back, her feet slipping on the damp stone floor. Her breath came in ragged gasps, each inhale a struggle against the overwhelming heaviness of the air. The walls of the chamber seemed to pulse with life, the roots and vines that clung to them twisting and shifting like something alive, sentient. She could feel the room closing in on her, the weight of centuries of secrets pressing in from every direction.

"No," Elara whispered, her voice trembling. "You're not him. You're not Daniel."

The figure did not answer, but his expression—if it could even be called an expression—twisted into something that could only be described as an almost pitying smile. The darkness around him seemed to deepen, thickening, pulling the very air from her lungs.

"Do you truly believe you have a choice?" he asked, the words laced with a cold, mocking tone. "You have always been part of this, Elara. You just never knew it. The blood that runs through your veins—it belongs to the Kingdom of Rain. You were always meant to come here. To us."

The room seemed to vibrate with the weight of his words, and Elara stumbled, her hands gripping the cold, slick stone wall for support. The images that had flashed through her mind earlier—the strange dreams, the visions of Marguerite—flooded back in a rush. She could feel the power of the Kingdom of Rain, an ancient force that had waited for centuries to be awakened. And now, she stood at the precipice, on the edge of something vast, something terrifying.

The figure of Daniel took a step forward, his eyes never leaving hers. "The power you feel in this place—it is yours, Elara. You only need to claim it."

Elara's hands clenched into fists. She refused to believe it. This—this wasn't her. She had never asked for this. The curse that had plagued her family, the secrets buried deep in her bloodline, they were not hers to own. She had fought too hard to be free of all of it. She had left her past behind her—why was it pulling her back now?

But the power in the room was undeniable. The pull was almost magnetic, tugging at her very soul, urging her to accept what was being offered. To join this twisted version of the life that had always been promised to her.

"No," Elara said again, her voice stronger now. "I will never be part of this."

For a moment, the figure—Daniel's doppelganger—paused, as if considering her words. The air grew colder, the shadows deeper. And then, with a sudden movement, the figure's hand shot out, grasping her wrist with an iron grip. Elara gasped, pain shooting up her arm, but she refused to let it show. She tried to pull away, but the grip was unyielding.

"You don't understand," the figure said, his voice low, almost pleading. "This is who you are. You cannot escape what is in your blood. You cannot run from your destiny."

His words echoed in the room, and Elara felt the weight of them pressing on her chest. She could feel the darkness closing in around her again, suffocating her, and she realized with a sickening jolt that he was right. She couldn't escape this place. She couldn't escape her bloodline. But she could fight. She could resist.

With all the strength she could muster, Elara twisted her wrist in the figure's grip, using her other hand to push against his chest. She shoved with everything she had, and for a brief moment, the figure faltered, taking a step back. The light in his eyes flickered, and in that instant, Elara saw something else—something human, something vulnerable beneath the facade.

For a split second, it was as though the figure of Daniel wavered, his true self threatening to break through the darkness that had consumed him. His features softened, his expression shifting into something closer to the man she had once known, before the darkness had taken him.

"Elara..." he whispered, and for a brief moment, his voice sounded like her Daniel's. But then, the mask returned, his face hardening again into that cold, inhuman expression. "You think you can fight this. You think you can resist. But you're wrong."

Before she could react, the room seemed to explode around her. The roots on the walls twisted violently, the vines shaking and recoiling as though in pain. The air hummed with energy, and Elara staggered back, her body shaking with the force of the moment. The floor trembled beneath her feet, and she felt a sharp pressure in the air, like the room itself was about to collapse.

"Elara, no!" a voice shouted, and for a brief, heart-stopping moment, she thought it was Daniel. But when she turned, her heart dropped.

It wasn't Daniel.

Marguerite stood at the far end of the chamber, her eyes glowing with a dark, unnatural light. Her presence filled the room like a storm, overwhelming, suffocating. The shadows seemed to grow thicker around her, curling and twisting like smoke. Her hands were outstretched, her fingers curled in an almost hypnotic way, as if she were casting some kind of spell.

"Elara, you've come so far," Marguerite said, her voice like silk, smooth and dangerous. "But it's too late. You can't escape what has been chosen for you."

The air in the room grew colder still, the darkness thicker, and Elara could feel the pull of the shadows growing stronger, tugging at her very soul. It was as though they were waiting for her to give in, to give herself over to whatever power Marguerite controlled.

"No..." Elara whispered, shaking her head violently. "I won't let you do this. I won't be a part of this."

Marguerite's smile stretched wider, her eyes gleaming with cruel satisfaction. "You think you have a choice?" she asked, taking a step closer. "You think you can fight destiny? The Kingdom of Rain does not allow for such weaknesses."

The words struck Elara like a physical blow, and for a moment, she felt her resolve falter. Was she truly powerless in all of this? Was she nothing more than a pawn in a game that had been played long before her birth?

But then—there, in the back of her mind—she heard it.

A whisper.

It wasn't the darkness, and it wasn't Marguerite's voice.

It was Daniel.

"Elara, you have to fight. Don't give up. You're stronger than this."

The words, soft yet filled with an undeniable urgency, jolted her back to herself. Her body surged with newfound strength, and she stepped forward, pushing past the overwhelming presence of the shadows. She turned her eyes back on Marguerite, no longer fearful, no longer uncertain.

"I am not yours," Elara said, her voice low but steady, her gaze unflinching. "I will never be yours."

Marguerite's expression faltered, just for a moment, before it twisted into something darker. "You will regret this."

But Elara didn't listen. She could feel the energy building in her, a power she didn't fully understand but that was unmistakably hers. She reached deep within herself, searching for the strength to fight, to break free from the curse that had haunted her bloodline.

The room trembled again, and as the shadows closed in around her, she made a choice.

It was time to break the cycle. Time to reclaim her life, her freedom, her future. Time to end the nightmare.

12

The Heart of the Storm

Elara's heart raced as she stood her ground, her hands shaking, her breath ragged. The shadows in the room seemed to pulse and writhe, feeding off the tension that crackled in the air. Marguerite's figure loomed in front of her, darker now, more menacing, but Elara refused to back down. She had felt it—the power, deep within herself, ready to break free. She couldn't let it slip away. Not now. Not after everything.

"You're wrong," Elara said, her voice steady despite the fear gnawing at her insides. "I'm not a puppet for you to control. I won't be part of your plan."

Marguerite's lips curled into a smile, but it wasn't one of amusement. It was cold, calculating, like a predator savoring the moment before the kill. Her eyes flickered with malice, glowing like two dark stars in the thickening gloom.

"You think you can resist me, Elara?" Marguerite purred, taking a deliberate step toward her. "You think you can escape your bloodline? The Kingdom of Rain will claim you, whether you fight or surrender. You have no idea what you're up against."

Elara swallowed hard, but she stood her ground, refusing to flinch. Her body ached with the weight of the dark magic around her, but deep inside, there was something stronger—something alive. A flicker of a long-forgotten power, buried deep within her soul. She could feel it, just beneath the surface, calling to her. And it was this power, this connection to the land, to her family's legacy, that she needed to tap into now, before Marguerite could fully unleash whatever dark plan she had set in motion.

"I'm not like you," Elara spat, her voice rising as the shadows around her seemed to react, the air growing heavier. "I will never be like you."

Marguerite's smile faltered for a fraction of a second, and in that moment, Elara knew she had struck a nerve. There was something deeply personal in what she had just said. Something that Marguerite wasn't ready to confront.

"You know nothing about me," Marguerite hissed, her hands clenched into fists. The shadows thickened around her, tendrils of darkness creeping toward Elara like serpents preparing to strike. "Nothing about what I've endured, the sacrifices I've made."

Elara narrowed her eyes. "Then tell me," she said, her voice calm but fierce. "Tell me what you think I should understand.

Tell me why I should be afraid of you."

Marguerite's eyes flashed with fury, and for the first time, there was a crack in her composed demeanor. She took another step forward, but this time, her voice dropped to a dangerous whisper, like the calm before a storm. "You don't know what it means to be a part of the Kingdom of Rain. The legacy, the power, the curse—it's all tied to you, Elara. It has always been tied to you."

The words sent a chill down Elara's spine, but she refused to back away. "You're wrong," she said, shaking her head. "I don't care about the Kingdom of Rain. I care about myself. I care about my life, my freedom. And I'm not going to let you take that from me."

Marguerite let out a low, menacing laugh. "You think you have a choice?" she asked. "You think you can walk away from all of this? You are already part of it. You always have been."

The air around Elara seemed to thicken, a pressure building in the room that threatened to crush her. She could feel it, the weight of centuries of magic, of blood, of destiny pressing in on her. But deep inside, a spark ignited. She wasn't going to let this woman—this monster—control her. Not now. Not ever.

With a sudden movement, Elara reached into herself, searching for that deep, buried connection to the land. She had always felt it, in the quiet of the rain, in the whisper of the wind through the trees, in the deep roots of the earth that held her family's legacy. It was there, pulsing beneath the surface, waiting for her to call upon it.

She could feel it now, growing stronger with every heartbeat, filling her veins with an energy she hadn't known was hers. The room around her seemed to grow quieter, as though the world itself was holding its breath. The shadows, the darkness—everything stilled, as if waiting for her to make her move.

"Elara..." Marguerite's voice was soft now, almost coaxing, but there was an underlying threat in it. "Stop. You don't know what you're doing. You can't control it."

But Elara wasn't listening. She felt it now, the power flowing through her like an electric current, charging her body, her soul. She could hear the whispers of the land, feel the rain running through her blood. She wasn't just a part of this legacy—she was its heir. And she would not let Marguerite twist that into something dark and evil.

"Enough!" Elara shouted, her voice ringing through the chamber like a clarion call.

With the force of her words, the shadows recoiled, as if repelled by the energy that radiated from her. The darkness in the room seemed to hesitate, pulling back, retreating from the strength of her will.

Marguerite's eyes widened with a mixture of shock and rage. "You can't do this," she growled, her voice low, guttural. "You don't understand—this isn't just about you. This is about all of us. The Kingdom of Rain needs its ruler, its queen. And that will be me."

Elara stood tall, her hands outstretched as she called on the power within her, the power that was hers by right. The floor beneath her feet began to vibrate, and she could feel the ground itself responding, the pulse of the land beneath her growing stronger. The air around her crackled with energy, the rain outside beginning to intensify, as if the heavens themselves were answering her call.

"You are not the queen," Elara said, her voice steady, even though her heart was pounding. "I am."

The ground trembled beneath her feet, and a blinding light flared from her hands, pushing the shadows back, forcing them to retreat. For a moment, the entire room was bathed in light, the roots and vines shuddering as the energy surged through them. The very walls of the chamber seemed to groan, as if the building itself was alive and responding to Elara's power.

Marguerite staggered back, her face contorted with fury, but Elara didn't falter. She could feel it now—the heart of the storm. The power that had always been hers, the power that had been passed down through generations, now surged to the surface. She had tapped into it. And there was no going back.

With one final cry, Elara thrust her hands forward, releasing the energy that had been building within her. The room shook violently, the air tearing with the force of her will. The roots and vines twisted and writhed as if in agony, their power bent to Elara's command. The shadows shrieked, retreating into the corners of the room as the light filled every inch of the space.

Marguerite screamed, her form flickering as if she were being torn apart by the force Elara had unleashed. The darkness around her swirled, thrashing in desperate resistance, but it was too late. Elara had taken control. She had broken free from the chains that had bound her for so long.

But even as the shadows fell back, even as the storm seemed to recede, Elara could feel the weight of what she had done. The power she had called upon—it was a double-edged sword. She could feel the land's pulse beneath her, the rain that had once been a comforting presence now a storm of chaos. The very earth itself seemed to tremble, its balance disturbed by the force she had unleashed.

Marguerite, her body contorted with fury, her hands reaching for Elara, screamed one last time before she disappeared into the shadows. The last remnants of her dark power dissipated, but Elara knew this wasn't over. It couldn't be. Not yet.

She stood alone in the center of the room, her hands still glowing with the energy she had summoned, her heart racing in her chest. The storm had broken, but the battle was far from over.

"Elara..." a voice whispered from the darkness, and her blood ran cold.

It was Daniel.

"Don't leave me…"

13

The Shattered Veil

Elara stood at the edge of the cliff, the wind howling through her hair, the sky above her a violent swirl of dark clouds and flashes of lightning. The storm, which had been nothing more than a whisper in the back of her mind for so long, now roared with a life of its own, filling the air with a crackling energy that matched the turmoil within her. She could feel its power rising, pushing against her, urging her to succumb to its embrace.

Her hand, the one that had once held the dagger so firmly, now trembled as it hung at her side. The weight of the weapon was no longer comforting—it was suffocating. Every moment that passed, every breath she took, felt like another step closer to losing herself entirely. She could hear it in the air—the whisper of the storm calling to her, telling her she was meant for something greater, something darker. Something she was beginning to fear.

"Elara," a voice called from behind her.

She didn't have to turn to know who it was. She would have known that voice anywhere. Daniel's voice, soft and steady, yet filled with a sense of urgency that she could not ignore. He had been with her through it all, from the very beginning of her journey to the storm's relentless arrival. But now, she wasn't sure how much longer he would stay.

Without looking at him, she spoke, her voice barely a whisper. "It's happening, Daniel. I can feel it. The storm... it's taking me."

She could hear his footsteps on the rocky ground as he approached, his presence like a calming force in the midst of the chaos. "It doesn't have to take you, Elara," he said, his voice full of resolve. "You have a choice. You always have."

A bitter laugh escaped her lips, sharp and hollow. "A choice? Look around you, Daniel. The storm is all I have left. It's too late for choices."

He stopped behind her, close enough that she could feel his warmth, but he didn't touch her. She didn't think she could bear it if he did. Not now. Not with the storm's cold breath on her skin, urging her to let go.

"Elara," he said again, this time his tone gentler, like he was reaching for something inside her. "You've always had the strength to choose your path. The storm doesn't control you unless you let it."

His words hit her like a wave, crashing against the walls she had built around her heart. She had always believed that the storm was the only thing she could control, the only thing that understood her. But now, standing on the edge of the abyss, Elara wasn't so sure anymore. The storm was a part of her, yes—but it was also consuming her, pulling her into its depths. She was slipping, and there was nothing she could do to stop it.

"Elara, please," Daniel urged, his voice breaking through her thoughts. "You can still fight it. You've always fought, always chosen to stand up when the world tried to tear you down. Don't let it win now."

His words were like a lifeline thrown into the storm, and for a moment, Elara thought she might reach out and grab it. But the storm was loud, deafening, its winds howling with fury. It was angry, relentless, as if it knew what was happening—knew that Elara was beginning to question her place in the world. She could feel the storm's grip tightening around her, pulling her toward the edge. The energy it gave her, the power she had once thought was her salvation, now felt like a poison coursing through her veins.

"I don't know who I am anymore, Daniel," she confessed, her voice trembling. "I used to think I was strong, that I could fight anything. But now... I'm losing myself. I can feel it, the storm changing me, turning me into something I don't recognize."

Daniel's silence was more than just the absence of words; it was the weight of his understanding. He had seen the change in her, the darkness that had slowly taken root in her heart. And yet, he didn't pull away. He didn't judge her. He stood there, patient, offering her the only thing he had left: his unwavering belief in her.

"You are more than the storm, Elara," he said softly. "You are the choice that makes you who you are. The storm is a part of you, but it doesn't define you."

The wind picked up, and Elara felt a shiver run through her. The storm was restless, sensing her internal conflict. It pushed against her, demanding that she surrender, that she embrace it completely. She could feel its hunger, the dark energy swirling inside her, tugging at her soul.

"No, Daniel," she said, her voice hoarse with pain. "I don't think I can fight it anymore."

He stepped forward, closing the distance between them. For

a moment, the storm seemed to quiet, as though even it was holding its breath, waiting to see what would happen next. His hand brushed against her arm, gentle but firm, and she flinched at the contact, her skin burning where he touched her. But he didn't pull away. He didn't retreat.

"Elara," he said, his voice low and steady, "I know you're afraid. I know the storm has taken so much from you. But you have the power to take it back. You can choose to stand against it, just like you've always stood against the odds."

She felt his words wrap around her like a shield, softening the edges of her fear. She wanted to believe him. She wanted to believe that she could still fight, that there was something left in her that could defy the storm's grip. But the deeper the storm reached into her, the harder it became to separate herself from its darkness.

"I don't know how, Daniel," she whispered, the tears she had been holding back finally slipping down her face. "I don't know how to fight anymore. I'm too far gone."

"You're not," he said firmly. "You've never been. You are stronger than you think, Elara. You've always had the strength to choose. And right now, you need to choose who you are."

The storm roared, a deafening cry that seemed to tear at her very soul. It was relentless, angry, and yet, in that moment, Elara could feel something else—a flicker of something, deep inside her. It was the spark of defiance, the same spark that had driven her to survive when everything else had crumbled. The storm had tried to take her, to turn her into something it could control, but it had underestimated her.

"Elara," Daniel said softly, his voice filled with a quiet desperation. "Please. Don't let the storm win."

The flicker grew stronger, and Elara took a deep breath. She closed her eyes for a moment, letting the storm's fury wash over her. She could feel it inside her, swirling and howling, but she was no longer afraid. The storm was powerful, yes, but it was not invincible. Not anymore.

With a sudden, sharp movement, Elara lifted her hand to the sky. The storm howled in fury, but she stood her ground. The power inside her, the power she had once feared, began to rise again—but this time, it was not the storm's power. It was hers. She could feel the pulse of the earth beneath her, the beat of her own heart syncing with the storm's rhythm.

"No more," she whispered, her voice carrying through the wind. "I choose."

The storm responded with a violent crash of thunder, but Elara stood firm, her eyes locked on the swirling darkness above her. She was no longer a victim of the storm. She was its master.

The veil had been shattered. The storm would no longer control her.

And for the first time in what felt like an eternity, Elara felt free.

14

The Edge of Eternity

Elara's breath hung in the air, thick with the weight of her decision. The room before her was shrouded in darkness, the corners creeping into the edges of her vision. The shadows felt more alive now, almost sentient, as if they had a mind of their own—drawing closer, pressing in on her.

She could still feel the surge of power in her veins, the echo of what she had done in the storm's wake. It was more than just a ripple in the fabric of the room. It was something far deeper, far more dangerous. She had severed the connection between herself and Marguerite, banishing the woman's dark influence from her mind, but that hadn't freed her completely.

The storm outside raged against the walls of the Kingdom of Rain. Thunder cracked like a whip, and the rain lashed against the windows in torrents. It felt like the world itself was weeping. Elara could feel the remnants of the magic still swirling around her, a constant undercurrent that threatened to pull her under. She had won this battle, but the war? That was still to come.

A whisper, barely audible, drifted to her ears.

"Elara..."

Her heart froze. It wasn't just the wind. It wasn't the storm outside. The voice, soft and beckoning, was something else entirely. Something more intimate. More familiar.

"Elara..." The voice was clearer now, and her breath caught in her throat.

It was Daniel.

Her mind reeled with the realization. Daniel's voice, fractured and distant, but unmistakable. Was it a trick of the mind? Or was he really there, calling to her from the edge of the world she had just fought to leave behind?

"Elara..."

The voice, though faint, was so real it sent a cold shiver down her spine. But it wasn't just his voice she could hear—it was something more, something almost physical. His presence lingered in the air, like a magnetic force pulling her toward it. The storm outside howled louder, and with every gust of wind, she could feel the storm's heart—the Kingdom of Rain—fighting to draw her back.

"Elara!" The voice was clearer, desperate, pained.

Her pulse quickened as her instincts screamed at her to run. But she couldn't. Not this time. There was something in Daniel's voice, something familiar in the way it trembled, that reached deep into her soul. It had been so long, so much had happened, but this voice—this was the man she had loved, the man she had fought for.

"Elara!" This time, it wasn't a whisper. It was an anguished cry that seemed to shake the very walls of the room.

Her feet moved before she could think, stepping away from the security of the doorway and toward the center of the room. The storm outside intensified, the wind slamming against the stone walls, rattling the windows as though the world was being torn apart. The air was thick with a haunting silence, punctuated only by the sound of her own heartbeat and the distant howling of the wind.

"Elara... please..."

A chill ran through her, but it wasn't the storm. It was something colder. Something darker.

"Daniel?" Elara called out, her voice hoarse as the air thickened around her.

The shadows that had been so still seemed to come alive, writhing and stretching across the room like a sea of blackness. The air grew thicker, heavier, and the oppressive weight of it pressed against her chest. The temperature plummeted, and Elara could see her breath in front of her as she shivered from the cold.

"Elara..." There it was again—his voice, rasping, strained with emotion. "I'm here."

A flicker of light flashed across her vision, and she turned toward it. The room had grown impossibly dark, but there, in the far corner, a faint glow began to pulse, weak but present. It beckoned to her, an invitation she couldn't ignore.

"Elara, you must come," Daniel's voice urged, now tinged with desperation. "You're running out of time."

Time? What was he talking about? Elara's mind swirled, trying to make sense of it all. She had to get to him. She had to find him, to rescue him from whatever had taken him. But the shadows—the darkness—surrounded her, pulling her deeper into the void.

The glow flickered again, and Elara's feet moved toward it. She reached out for the light, her heart pounding in her chest. The shadows retreated as she advanced, but they did not vanish. They seemed to watch her, to follow her every move.

"Daniel... where are you?" she whispered, barely daring to speak the words aloud.

A soft, almost imperceptible whisper answered her: "Here."

Her hands trembled as she reached for the source of the light. The warmth of it was a comfort, but it was fleeting, ephemeral, like a dream slipping away upon waking. And then, there he was.

Daniel.

He stood in front of her, his form shimmering in the dim light. He was there, yet not entirely real. His edges blurred like smoke, fading in and out of focus, his features shifting, as if the very fabric of his being was unraveling. His eyes—those deep, soulful eyes—met hers, filled with an unbearable sorrow, a pain so intense it nearly brought her to her knees.

"Elara..." His voice broke, soft and full of longing. "Please... don't leave me."

She reached for him, her hands trembling, but as her fingers brushed his arm, it was like grasping at mist. His form rippled like water, and for a moment, she wasn't sure if he was even truly there. But his voice—his voice, so real and desperate—continued to echo in her mind.

"Don't let me go," he begged. "You're the only one who can save me."

Elara's heart clenched painfully in her chest. Save him? How could she save him when she wasn't even sure if he was real? How could she pull him from the shadows that seemed to devour him, from the very realm he was trapped in?

"Daniel, what happened?" she asked, her voice barely a whisper as she fought against the cold, the heavy feeling of dread that clung to the air around them.

He took a step closer, his form solidifying for just a moment.

But as he did, the shadows surged, pulling at him, trying to drag him back. His face twisted with agony, and for the first time since she had heard his voice, Elara saw fear in his eyes.

"I—I can't escape," Daniel stammered, his voice strained. "It's too late, Elara. The Kingdom of Rain—it's too strong. It won't let me go."

The words hit her like a physical blow. The Kingdom of Rain. Of course. The kingdom that had haunted her family for generations. The very thing that had tried to pull her into its depths. And now it had taken Daniel. It had taken him, and it wouldn't let him go.

Elara's mind raced. There had to be a way. There had to be something she could do to break the hold of the kingdom's power. She couldn't lose him. Not like this.

"Daniel, please," she whispered, her voice breaking. "I won't let them have you. I won't let them take you from me."

His form flickered again, fading and reappearing, his outline growing fainter with every passing second. The darkness around him was closing in, suffocating him. She could feel it, the heavy pressure of the kingdom's magic, pressing against her from all sides.

"Elara… you're the key," Daniel's voice rasped, barely audible now. "You're the only one who can stop this. You have to finish what you started. You have to break the kingdom's hold… for both of us."

His voice was fading, and with it, the light that had been surrounding him. Elara reached out, her hands trembling as she tried to grasp him once more, but he slipped through her fingers like smoke.

"Daniel!" she cried, her heart shattering.

And then, in a final, desperate whisper, his voice was gone.

"Elara…"

The silence that followed was deafening.

Elara stood alone in the room, her breath shallow, her hands still outstretched, empty.

The storm outside raged on.

15

The Weight of Silence

Elara stood frozen, her hands still reaching out, grasping at the remnants of Daniel's voice. The air around her was thick, pressing in from all sides, and the room had grown unbearably quiet. The distant sounds of the storm outside had faded into an eerie stillness, leaving behind only the harsh rhythm of her own breath. She felt as though the world had shifted, the very ground beneath her unstable, like a tremor had rattled the foundation of reality itself.

Daniel's voice... that faint whisper, calling to her from the depths, was gone. The darkness had claimed him, dragging him back into the shadows, into the heart of the Kingdom of Rain. She could still feel the pull of it, that intangible weight, like a rope pulling her toward the edge of a chasm.

"He's gone," she whispered to herself, her voice trembling. It wasn't a question. It was a stark, painful truth that settled like a stone in her chest.

But even as the words left her lips, she couldn't bring herself to believe them. She couldn't accept it. The feeling, the pull of his presence, was still there, faint but undeniable. She could sense it, like a flickering candle in the distance, waiting for her to reach it, to rescue him from whatever nightmare he was trapped in.

She took a step forward, but her legs felt heavy, as though they were rooted to the floor. The shadows seemed to grow, stretching toward her, curling around her feet like fingers trying to pull her down. The air grew colder, and Elara's breath came out in visible puffs. It wasn't just the temperature—this chill was something else, something darker.

The Kingdom of Rain. The words echoed in her mind, over and over, like a taunting mantra. That cursed place had taken Daniel, and she knew it would stop at nothing to claim her as well. She had defied it once, had struck at its core, but that had been only the beginning. She had uncovered its power, felt its reach—but she hadn't destroyed it. She hadn't severed its hold on the world. And as long as the kingdom's grip remained, Daniel's fate was sealed.

She couldn't bear it. She couldn't let him be lost to that shadowy realm, not when she still had a chance to save him.

"Elara," a voice suddenly called, so soft it barely broke the air. But it was enough.

Her heart leaped, her pulse spiking. She turned toward the sound, her eyes wide, scanning the room for any sign of movement, any trace of life. The voice, familiar but distant, called to her again.

"Elara."

It was Daniel. His voice. But no… not again. It couldn't be. She had just heard it fading, lost in the shadows. He was gone.

And yet, there it was again, sharp and clear, as if he were standing right in front of her.

"Elara, you must listen to me."

This time, the voice was more insistent, more real. She could feel it, resonating in her chest, in the very air around her. This wasn't some fleeting whisper. This was him, reaching out from beyond, reaching through the storm.

"Elara!" the voice cried again, desperate, almost frantic. "You must come. You must stop it, before it's too late."

"Elara!" the voice begged once more, louder now, more tangible, pulling at her with such force she couldn't ignore it. Her legs moved before she could think, the energy rushing through her body as she took a step forward. Another.

"Elara…" The voice was more than just a call now. It was a command, a plea she couldn't disregard. She felt his presence, palpable in the air, and she moved faster, her steps sure as she followed the sound of his voice.

But as she moved, the shadows grew darker, thicker, like a smothering blanket. The room shifted around her, walls warping, reality bending under the weight of some unseen force. Elara's breath quickened, panic rising as she tried to focus, to center herself on the sound of Daniel's voice.

"Elara, you have to hurry!" His voice was near now, but just as her fingers reached out to grasp it, it vanished. Silence swallowed the room again, leaving her standing in the dark, heart pounding, her outstretched hand trembling.

She stopped dead in her tracks. This was a trap. It had to be. The Kingdom of Rain was toying with her. The shadows were pulling at her, mocking her, showing her what she longed for only to rip it away again.

"Elara…" The voice came again, quieter now. It was weak, like a dying breath.

The ground beneath her shifted, and she stumbled, catching herself against the cold stone wall. The room seemed to close in on her, the walls pressing tighter, as if the very air was turning against her. Every breath she took felt labored, thick with the heaviness of the magic that hung in the space.

"Elara…"

Her knees buckled, and she dropped to the floor, her hands gripping the cold stone for support. She couldn't breathe. She couldn't think. The air was suffocating, the shadows closing in around her. She wanted to run, to flee from the darkness that threatened to swallow her, but her body wouldn't obey.

And then, in the stillness, something shifted.

A flicker. A movement. A shadow that seemed to slide just beyond her sight.

She turned, her heart skipping a beat. For a moment, she thought she saw something in the corner of the room—a figure, cloaked in shadow, barely visible but unmistakable.

"Elara..." It was him again. Daniel.

She stood up, her pulse racing as she forced herself toward the figure, but as she approached, it seemed to dissolve, fading into the air like mist. And again, she was left alone, in the silence, with only the echo of his voice ringing in her ears.

The silence stretched on, and the darkness seemed to press even closer, suffocating her. The room felt like a tomb, each breath she took more labored than the last.

"Elara..." This time, the voice was different—softer, weaker, but no less insistent. "Please..."

The word wrenched at her heart. She couldn't do this. She couldn't keep playing this game with the shadows. They were pulling her in, luring her with false promises, and she was losing herself in the process.

"No more," Elara whispered, her voice trembling as she steadied herself. "I can't keep chasing you... this isn't real."

But as she spoke the words, she felt it. A presence—subtle but undeniable—behind her, a shift in the air. She turned slowly, almost afraid of what she might see, and there he was.

Daniel.

He stood just a few feet away, his figure flickering like a dying candle. He looked the same as he had the last time she saw him—his dark hair falling over his brow, his eyes bright with emotion—but there was something wrong, something... off about him. His form shimmered in the dim light, fading at the edges, as if he were a dream teetering on the edge of reality.

"Elara," he said again, his voice strained, laced with a deep, aching sorrow. "You have to listen to me. You have to stop it. It's the only way..."

He reached toward her, his hand trembling, but as she stepped forward, the light around him seemed to flicker and die, and once again, he disappeared.

Elara stumbled back, a sharp gasp escaping her lips. She couldn't breathe. She couldn't think. Every time she reached for him, he slipped away, fading into nothingness. The Kingdom of Rain was playing with her, drawing her further into its web of lies.

But Daniel's voice still echoed in her mind. His words, still so vivid, so clear—"You have to stop it. It's the only way..."

There was a choice here. A choice she had to make. She could chase him, follow the echoes of his voice deeper into the darkness, and allow herself to be swallowed by the storm. Or she could face what lay ahead and fight, fight for him, for the kingdom, for everything that was worth saving.

Her heart thundered in her chest as she made her decision.

She wasn't going to lose him again.

"Elara..." The voice called once more, but this time, it was different. It was real. And it was up to her to decide whether she could reach him before it was too late.

Her feet moved forward.

She stepped into the unknown.

16

The Heart of the Storm

The Kingdom of Rain had a pulse. Elara felt it now, beneath the cold stone beneath her feet, in the deep thrum of the wind that howled through the cracks of the castle. It was like a living thing, ancient and powerful, pulling at her from all sides. A steady rhythm, as if it were breathing. As if it were waiting.

The air had grown even heavier, thick with a charged energy that made every breath feel like an effort. She could feel it in her chest, in the air swirling around her, the same energy that had clung to the very walls of the kingdom. This was where it began, and here was where it would end. If she failed here, she would be lost to the same darkness that had consumed Daniel, consumed everything she had once known.

"Elara…" His voice cut through the tension like a blade, soft but undeniably real. It was close now, so close she could almost touch it. The edge of her mind sharpened, every fiber of her being focused on finding him, saving him, pulling him back from the abyss.

She had followed the whispers, the fading traces of his voice, deeper into the heart of the castle, and now she was standing in the great hall, where the storm outside could no longer reach her. The vast room stretched endlessly before her, its ceiling lost in shadow, its walls etched with strange symbols that twisted like living things.

Her heart hammered in her chest as she stepped forward, every footfall a pulse in the growing silence.

"Daniel?" Her voice trembled as she called out, but the sound echoed back to her, hollow and empty, as though the castle itself was swallowing her words. She was alone—or was she?

"Elara…" The voice was unmistakable now, rising from the depths, curling around her like smoke, tugging at her senses. It was him. But his voice, though familiar, was no longer the man she loved. It was distorted, darkened, warped by the very air that surrounded them.

"Elara, you must listen…" His voice broke, the desperation in it enough to bring her to her knees. But she could not let him go. She would not. Not when she was this close. She had come this far, fought so hard to escape the shadow of this place, to resist the pull of the kingdom. She couldn't stop now.

"Elara…" The voice faltered, weak as though it were coming from far away.

"Daniel!" She cried out, her heart in her throat. "Where are you?"

The room seemed to grow colder as if the shadows themselves were creeping toward her. The wind outside howled like a wolf in the distance, but here, inside, there was only silence—complete, suffocating silence.

A flicker of movement in the corner of her vision caught her attention. She turned sharply, but there was nothing there, just the empty stone walls stretching out into the void.

"Elara..." His voice again. This time, it was not a whisper. It was stronger, coming from a place closer—so close she could almost feel his breath against her ear.

The hair on the back of her neck stood on end as she spun around, the shadows swirling in response. She had known, deep down, that this moment was coming, that the kingdom would test her resolve, drag her into its depths before she could claim victory.

"Elara, you don't have much time..." His words faltered, and for a brief, horrifying second, Elara thought she heard something break in his voice. "It's too late for me..."

"No." She shook her head, the word escaping her lips before she could stop it. "It's not too late. I won't lose you."

The shadows seemed to pulse, to ripple as she spoke. The air thickened again, charged with an energy so palpable she could almost touch it. She stepped forward, towards the center of the room, where the darkness seemed deepest, where the pull of the kingdom was strongest.

"Elara, you don't understand," Daniel's voice came again, softer, more distant. "I'm already gone."

"No." Elara's voice broke. "I can feel you, Daniel. I can still hear you. You're not gone."

His voice trembled on the wind. "You don't know what it's like here... It's not just shadows, Elara. It's everything. It's the very heart of this place, and I... I'm losing myself. I can't fight it any longer."

Her chest tightened, her heart aching as she understood the weight of his words. The Kingdom of Rain didn't just take lives—it consumed them. It twisted them, reshaping them until nothing of the person who had once been remained. It made them part of itself, and once it had them, it would never let go.

But she couldn't, wouldn't accept that. She couldn't let it claim Daniel. Not when he was so close. Not when he was still calling out to her.

"Please, don't give up," she whispered, her voice trembling. "I won't stop. I won't leave you."

For a long moment, there was only silence. The storm outside raged on, but here, in the heart of the kingdom, the quiet was suffocating. Elara felt the weight of it press down on her like a vice. Every breath she took felt harder than the last. The shadows shifted, stretching and pulling toward her, as if they were alive—alive and hungry.

"Elara, listen to me," Daniel's voice broke through the quiet once again. But this time, it wasn't just his voice. There was something else—something darker—woven into it. "You have to go. You can't win this fight. You don't understand what this place does to people."

A chill ran down her spine as she stood there, frozen, unsure of what to do. He was right in front of her now, so close she could feel his presence, but still just out of reach. His form flickered like a ghost, shifting and distorting in the dim light, and Elara realized with a sinking feeling that the shadows weren't just around her—they were inside him, pulling at his soul.

"No," she whispered, her throat tightening. "I won't leave you. I can't."

"Elara..." His voice faltered. "I'm... not the person you remember."

Her heart stopped. The words sliced through her, deep and raw. She could feel the truth in them, feel the heavy weight of it, and for a split second, she almost believed it. Almost.

But then she remembered the promise she had made, the promise to herself, to him, to the world. She wasn't going to give up. Not now, not when she was so close.

"No," she repeated, louder this time, stronger. "I don't believe you. You're still here. I can still feel you. I can still hear you. I won't let the kingdom take you."

The shadows around her writhed, and the temperature in the room dropped, a coldness creeping into her bones as the kingdom pressed harder, its influence bearing down on her.

"Elara..." Daniel's voice was more distant now, the words laced with a sense of finality. "You have to stop. You don't have much time. The kingdom—"

The ground beneath her feet shook, and the walls of the room seemed to close in, the stones creaking and groaning under the weight of some unseen force. She stumbled back, her hands reaching for something, anything to steady herself, but there was nothing. The world was spinning, the shadows closing in tighter with every passing second.

"Elara..." Daniel's voice, so faint now, whispered one last time. "Please. Don't let it consume you."

And then, the room went silent. The shadows pulled away, retreating into the corners of the room, leaving Elara standing alone in the heart of the storm.

For a long moment, everything was still.

But the storm outside raged on. The kingdom had not let go.

17

The Breaking Point

Elara's breath was shallow as she stood in the center of the cold stone room, her body trembling from the weight of the silence that had fallen over her. The shadows had retreated, but the air was thick with the remnants of their presence, like smoke that had settled into every crevice, every corner. Her mind was racing, her heart pounding in her chest as the reality of what had just happened began to sink in.

Daniel was gone. Not just lost, not just hidden in the depths of the Kingdom of Rain, but consumed. His voice, once so close, had faded into nothing, leaving behind only an emptiness that echoed through her very soul. She had heard him, had felt him, but now... now there was nothing. The Kingdom had won.

"No..." she whispered, her voice trembling, as if speaking the words aloud might somehow change the truth of them. "No, I won't accept that."

She took a step forward, then another, but her legs felt like lead.

Every step she took, the ground seemed to give way beneath her, and she had to steady herself against the wall to keep from collapsing. The energy in the room was thick, suffocating, as though the very air was pressing against her, refusing to let her move, to let her think.

The storm outside had grown louder, the wind howling through the cracks in the walls, its fury mirrored by the pounding in her head. She could feel the storm's presence, feel the pull of it, like a magnet drawing her closer. It was as though the storm, the Kingdom itself, was alive, watching her, waiting for her to make a choice.

She couldn't stay here. Not in this room, not in this place. But where would she go? What could she do? Every path she had taken had led her deeper into the heart of the storm, deeper into the heart of the Kingdom. It had trapped her here, just as it had trapped Daniel.

Her hand reached for the cold stone walls, seeking something—anything—to hold on to. But there was nothing. Nothing except the shadows that continued to pulse around her, their movement like the rhythm of a beating heart. It was as though the room itself was alive, breathing, waiting for her to make her next move.

"Elara…"

The voice.

Her heart stopped.

For a moment, she didn't dare to breathe, afraid that if she moved, if she made a sound, the voice would vanish as quickly as it had appeared. But then it came again, clearer this time, though still faint, like a whisper carried on the wind.

"Elara... Please..."

It was Daniel. His voice. But it was different now, somehow. There was a strange undertone to it, a heaviness that had not been there before, a darkness that pulled at the edges of her mind.

"Elara..." he repeated, his voice breaking through the silence like a plea. "You have to help me. You have to stop it."

The words struck her like a blow to the chest, and Elara's hands shot up to her mouth, her breath catching in her throat. She felt the pull of the voice, a magnetic force that dragged her forward, toward the source of the sound. Her body moved before she could think, her legs carrying her across the room, her feet almost slipping on the smooth stone floor.

"Elara..."

She turned sharply, her heart pounding in her ears. His voice had come from behind her, from the far corner of the room, but when she turned, there was nothing there. Just darkness. Just shadows that seemed to stretch endlessly, swallowing everything in their path.

"Elara, please..."

The voice was closer now. She could feel it, vibrating in the very air around her, pulling at her senses. The darkness seemed to twist, to swirl, and for a moment, she thought she saw something move within it—something that wasn't quite real, but also not entirely gone.

"Daniel?" Her voice was breathless, her hands trembling as she reached out, searching for him in the gloom. "Where are you?"

"Elara... help me..."

The words were faint now, barely a whisper, as though they were being carried away by the storm, lost in the wind. Elara's chest tightened, a deep sense of dread rising in her throat. She could feel the air thickening around her, the very walls of the room closing in, as though the Kingdom was trying to swallow her whole.

"Elara, you don't have much time..."

The voice came again, but this time it was different. There was a harshness to it now, a coldness that made Elara freeze in her tracks. It was no longer the voice she had known, no longer the voice of the man she loved. It was something else, something twisted and wrong.

Her stomach lurched as the shadows seemed to pulse, their movement like a living thing, reaching out toward her, pulling her into their depths. She had to move. She had to get out.

"Elara..." The voice came again, but this time it was a growl, a low, guttural sound that echoed in the room. It sent a jolt of fear through her, and for a moment, she hesitated, unsure of what to do. The Kingdom was shifting around her, the walls distorting, the very air growing thicker, suffocating her.

"Elara..."

Her breath caught in her throat as the voice grew louder, more insistent. It was no longer Daniel's voice. It was something darker, something more sinister, and it sent a wave of cold dread through her. It was pulling at her, trying to drag her into the heart of the storm, into the heart of the Kingdom.

"Elara, you don't understand..." The voice laughed, a cruel, mocking sound that echoed in her mind. "You were never meant to leave. This is where you belong."

The shadows swirled around her, closing in, and Elara stumbled backward, her heart racing. Her hand shot out, grasping for anything to steady herself, but there was nothing. The darkness was consuming her, drawing her deeper into its grip.

"No," she gasped, shaking her head, her voice shaking with terror. "No, I won't... I won't let you take me."

But the shadows pressed in tighter, their grip tightening around her like chains. She could feel their cold fingers brushing against her skin, their whispers brushing against her mind, threatening to pull her under.

"Elara..." The voice again, but this time, it was not just one voice. It was many, overlapping, blending together into a single, chilling chorus. "You cannot fight it. You cannot escape. You were always meant to be a part of us."

The words echoed through her, filling her mind with terror. The Kingdom was alive, and it had claimed her, claimed her soul. There was no escaping it.

"No!" Elara screamed, her voice filled with panic. "I won't become part of you! I won't..."

Her hands reached out, desperately searching for something— anything to pull her free. She couldn't let it take her. Not after everything. Not after all she had fought for.

And then, as if in answer to her cries, something in the darkness shifted.

A light.

It was faint at first, just a glimmer in the corner of her vision, but as Elara turned toward it, the light grew brighter, more solid. The shadows recoiled from it, as though the light was something they feared.

The pull of the darkness lessened, just enough for Elara to take a breath, to steady herself. The light grew brighter still, and with it, the darkness began to fade.

"Elara..."

The voice again, but this time, it was Daniel's voice. Real. Strong. The shadows no longer reached for her.

"Elara..." His voice was clear now, no longer distorted by the darkness, no longer a whisper. He was here.

She turned, her heart racing as the light grew even brighter. In the center of it stood Daniel, his form solid and real, his eyes filled with a mixture of pain and hope.

"Elara, you have to stop it," he said, his voice urgent. "Before it's too late."

But the Kingdom was still there, its darkness swirling, waiting for the next moment of weakness. And Elara knew, deep down, that the fight was far from over.

18

The Reckoning

The light flickered, dimming and brightening like the pulse of a dying star, its warmth growing stronger, almost unbearable. Elara stood frozen, her heart hammering as she looked at Daniel, his form emerging from the swirling darkness like a beacon. It was him—she could feel it, deep down, in the very marrow of her bones. But something was different. His eyes were hollow, a shadow of the man she remembered, and the air around him seemed to hum with a malevolent energy, an almost suffocating heaviness that she couldn't ignore.

"Elara..." His voice cracked, as though he had been calling her for eternity, his words breaking through the tension in the room. His expression was torn—pained, but with a glimmer of something deeper, something she could not quite place. It was as if he were fighting with himself, a battle raging just beneath the surface of his calm, pleading gaze.

"You're here," she whispered, her voice trembling, her body rigid with the weight of what this moment could mean. "I can still save you."

He shook his head slowly, his lips curling into a faint, sorrowful smile, though it didn't quite reach his eyes. "Elara… no one can save me now."

"No!" The word left her before she could stop it, sharp and desperate. "I've come this far. I won't lose you. Not to this place. Not to the Kingdom."

The air thickened again, wrapping itself around her like a suffocating blanket, the weight of the room pressing down on her chest. The shadows on the walls seemed to lean in closer, watching, waiting, as if they were eager to see whether she would succeed or fail.

Daniel took a step back, and Elara immediately reached out, her hand trembling as she tried to close the distance between them. But the space between them seemed to stretch, a yawning chasm that she couldn't cross.

"Elara, you don't understand," he said, his voice trembling now, the rawness in his tone betraying the fragility of his resolve. "The Kingdom—this place—it doesn't just take lives. It takes who we are. It twists us into something… something that's not even human anymore."

The walls seemed to thrum with the truth of his words, the darkness around them pulsing in rhythm with his voice, as though it were alive, feeding off the very essence of his words. Elara felt a chill crawl up her spine, but she refused to step back.

She couldn't afford to—couldn't let him slip further away from her.

"I don't care," she whispered fiercely. "I won't let it take you. I'll fight. I'll find a way."

"You can't fight it," Daniel replied, his voice tight. "It's already taken me, Elara. I've lost myself to it. You can't fight something that's become part of you. It's everywhere. It's in the very air, in the stone of the castle, in the blood that flows through your veins. You can't run from it. You can't escape it."

Elara shook her head, forcing herself to take a deep breath, grounding herself in the present, in the fight that lay ahead. She wouldn't accept this. Not now, not after everything they had been through.

"Maybe you're right," she said quietly, her voice filled with an eerie calm that she didn't entirely recognize. "Maybe I can't fight it. But I can't give up on you. I won't let this Kingdom—this thing—win."

As she spoke the words, the shadows seemed to recoil, a low rumble vibrating through the floor beneath her. The temperature in the room plummeted, the air growing colder with every passing second, until her breath formed small clouds before her. She shivered, but her gaze never wavered from Daniel, even though she could feel the malevolent force of the Kingdom growing stronger, more oppressive.

"Elara..." Daniel's voice was barely audible now, distorted and breaking, as though he was struggling to hold on to his own sanity. "You don't understand. I've already made the choice."

Elara's heart skipped a beat. "What choice? What do you mean?"

The silence that followed was suffocating, and for a moment, Elara thought he wasn't going to answer. But then, his eyes flickered—something dark behind them, a flicker of recognition, of the man he had once been, before it was smothered by the shadows once again.

"I chose to stay," he said finally, his voice distant, almost hollow. "I chose to remain here, with the Kingdom. I let it take me. Because it's the only way I could... survive."

Her breath caught in her throat. "Survive?"

"The Kingdom doesn't just kill, Elara," Daniel continued, his voice gaining strength. "It reshapes. It redefines. It gives power. The power to survive. And that's all I've ever wanted—to survive. The rest... the rest of me... it's gone. I can't even remember what it was like before. But here..." He looked down, his eyes flickering to the floor. "Here, I'm more than I ever was. More powerful than I could have imagined."

The words sank into her like a blade, the reality of them slicing through the hope that had been burning so brightly in her chest. Was this it? Was Daniel truly lost? Was the man she loved no longer there, consumed by the Kingdom, its power too great to resist?

She reached for him again, this time desperate, her hand outstretched, but the space between them had grown farther, the air thick with an invisible force pushing her away.

"Daniel," she whispered, tears threatening to fall, her voice breaking under the weight of her own pain. "Please... don't do this. You're not a part of this place. You don't belong to it. You belong to me."

A flicker of something crossed his face then—a shadow of the man she had once known, the man who had laughed with her, loved her, fought by her side. But it was fleeting, like a dream fading on the edge of consciousness. And then it was gone.

"I'm not yours anymore," he said, his voice cold, final. "You have to leave. There's nothing left for you here."

The room seemed to pulse with a dark rhythm, the air vibrating with the oppressive weight of the Kingdom's power. Elara's hands clenched into fists at her sides, her nails digging into her palms as she fought against the overwhelming sense of helplessness threatening to overtake her.

"No..." she whispered again, her voice low but filled with a fierce defiance. "I'm not leaving. Not without you."

The darkness responded, thickening, swirling around her like an endless tide, the shadows closing in on her, as though the Kingdom was intent on smothering her, dragging her into its depths.

"Elara," Daniel said, his voice soft, a trace of regret creeping into the words. "You don't know what you're asking. You don't know the cost."

"Then tell me," she cried, stepping forward, the force of her will overcoming the weight of the shadows pressing in on her. "Tell me what I need to do to bring you back. I'll do anything. Just tell me."

The darkness quivered, its pulse erratic, but Daniel didn't speak again. Instead, his eyes seemed to harden, the last vestige of humanity fading behind the shadow that had consumed him.

"Elara..." he whispered, his voice barely audible now, so low it was almost lost in the growing roar of the storm outside. "You should have never come. The Kingdom doesn't forgive. It doesn't let go."

And then, with a sudden, almost imperceptible movement, Daniel stepped back, vanishing into the swirling darkness of the room.

"No!" Elara shouted, reaching out in a futile attempt to catch him, but he was already gone. The room was empty, save for the shadows that now pressed in tighter, the storm outside growing louder, more violent.

She stood alone.

But even as the Kingdom of Rain closed in around her, something inside her snapped. She couldn't—wouldn't—let this be the end. Not for Daniel. Not for herself.

The fight had only just begun.

19

the Storm

Elara stood motionless, the cold wind howling through the cracks in the stone walls. Her breath came in ragged gasps, the chill of the air seeping deep into her bones. The storm outside had intensified, as if it, too, were reacting to the chaos inside the castle. The very walls seemed to groan under the weight of the wind, the timbers creaking and groaning as though they might collapse at any moment. But it wasn't the storm that had her attention—it was the feeling that the Kingdom of Rain was closing in on her.

Daniel was gone. She had felt him slip away, like sand through her fingers, vanishing into the shadows of the Kingdom. She could still hear his voice, faint in her mind, calling her back. But the man she loved was no longer there. What was left of him had been swallowed by the darkness, twisted into something she could hardly recognize.

And yet, she refused to let him go. The Kingdom had taken so much from her, from them both, but she wasn't about to let it take Daniel too. There had to be a way to break its hold. There had to be a way to save him—before it was too late.

Her eyes darted across the room, searching for any sign of movement, any indication that she wasn't truly alone. But there was nothing—just the oppressive stillness of the stone walls, the deafening roar of the storm outside, and the distant whisper of the shadows, as though the Kingdom itself were watching her, waiting for her next move.

The wind rattled the windows, shaking the fragile glass, and Elara flinched at the sound. Her fingers clenched around the hilt of the dagger at her side, her only remaining weapon against the overwhelming forces around her. She had to be ready for whatever came next.

Suddenly, a low growl rippled through the room, vibrating in the floor beneath her. Elara's heart skipped a beat as the darkness seemed to pulse with a life of its own. The shadows writhed, swirling around the room like tendrils of smoke, and she instinctively took a step back, her eyes wide as she searched for the source of the sound.

"Elara…"

The voice.

It was his voice. Daniel's voice, but it was distorted, torn and twisted by the darkness that surrounded them. The sound of it sent a shiver down her spine, her skin crawling as if the very air were turning against her.

"Daniel?" she whispered, her voice thick with fear and desperation.

The darkness shifted, a faint glow emerging from the far corner of the room. Elara's eyes narrowed, her heart pounding in her chest as she slowly moved toward it, the light drawing her in like a moth to a flame. It flickered and wavered, as though it, too, were struggling to hold its ground against the oppressive weight of the shadows.

"Elara..." The voice came again, this time sharper, more insistent. "You have to stop. It's too late."

She reached the corner, her breath catching in her throat as she found the source of the light. It was a small, glowing orb, hovering just above the ground. But the moment her fingers brushed against it, the orb flickered, and the room seemed to lurch beneath her feet.

The shadows surged forward, thick and black, engulfing the orb and pulling it into the darkness. Elara stumbled back, her heart racing, but before she could react, the room exploded with a sound that was half a roar, half a scream—a terrifying, guttural sound that seemed to shake the very foundations of the castle.

"Elara..."

The voice again, but this time, it wasn't Daniel's. It was something deeper, something older. The voice of the Kingdom itself, speaking through the shadows, speaking through the storm.

"You cannot escape me," the voice growled, the words reverberating through the stone walls. "You are mine. All of you."

The shadows surged forward again, faster this time, and Elara barely had time to draw her dagger before they were upon her, wrapping around her legs like chains, dragging her toward the center of the room. The darkness was cold—colder than anything she had ever felt—like the chill of the grave itself, and the grip of it was unrelenting.

"Elara, don't fight it," the voice whispered, almost tender, as if it were offering her a bargain. "Join me. Let me make you whole again."

She gasped as the darkness tightened its hold, cutting off her breath, choking her. The voice in her mind was everywhere, the Kingdom's whispers weaving through her thoughts, making it harder and harder to hold onto her sanity. Images of Daniel flashed in her mind—his face, his eyes, his voice. But the more she thought of him, the more the shadows seemed to twist, the more the room seemed to pulse with malevolent energy.

"No..." she choked out, forcing the words past the constriction in her chest. "I won't let you have me."

Her fingers tightened around the dagger, and with all the strength she could muster, she slashed at the shadows, the blade cutting through the air with a sickening hiss. The shadows recoiled, but only for a moment before surging forward again, stronger, more insistent.

"Let go," the voice crooned, now a low, seductive murmur. "It's not worth fighting. There is no escape. You belong to me now."

Her pulse thudded in her ears, the storm outside drowning out everything else, the wind howling through the castle, as though it, too, was trying to warn her. The room was spinning, the shadows swirling around her, dragging her deeper into the heart of the storm. The Kingdom was alive, and it wanted her. It wanted all of her.

But Elara's resolve was iron. She had come this far, fought too long, to let the darkness claim her now.

With a ferocity born of desperation, she thrust the dagger into the darkness, the blade sinking into something solid. The shadows screamed—a high-pitched, horrible sound that rattled her bones—and for a moment, the room seemed to stop. The pressure around her chest loosened, the darkness withdrawing just enough for her to breathe.

"Elara..."

It was Daniel's voice again, but this time, it wasn't distorted. It wasn't broken. It was the voice she remembered, the voice she had fought so hard to save. Her heart surged in her chest, hope flickering like a fragile flame.

"Elara, you have to leave," Daniel's voice said, this time desperate. "It's not you they want. It's me. I am the one they need. Please, don't let the Kingdom take you too."

The shadows shuddered violently, the room shaking with the force of their struggle. The walls groaned, as if the entire castle were being torn apart by the power of the storm. The very air seemed to tremble with the energy of the Kingdom, the storm's fury mirrored by the chaos inside.

"I won't leave you," Elara gasped, fighting to stay on her feet. The shadows were receding, but they were not gone. Not yet. "I'm not leaving you."

"Elara..." Daniel's voice came again, softer now, almost pleading. "You don't understand. It's already too late for me."

The shadows around her thickened again, twisting tighter, wrapping around her in an almost affectionate embrace. It was as if the Kingdom itself were cradling her in its arms, coaxing her into surrender.

But Elara couldn't give up. Not when Daniel was still out there. She wouldn't let him be consumed by the darkness. She couldn't.

She clenched the dagger in her hand, her knuckles white, and slashed it through the shadows again. The dark tendrils recoiled, and for a moment, the light in the room flickered, then steadied.

"Elara..." Daniel's voice wavered, as if it were fading, lost in the tumult of the storm. "Please... run."

But Elara was already moving, already running toward the source of the light, toward the heart of the storm. The Kingdom of Rain could not break her. It could not defeat her.

She would fight for him.

And somehow, she would find a way to destroy the Kingdom itself.

The storm was only beginning. And so, too, was her fight.

20

The Threshold

The castle was alive with noise—too much noise, too much motion. Elara could feel it all around her, the air thick with the sense of something ancient, something malicious waking from a deep, restless sleep. She could hear it in the creaking of the stone walls, the way the storm outside howled in sync with the growling shadows inside. The Kingdom of Rain was shifting, its power stirring, and Elara, for the first time since she'd arrived, felt a tremor of doubt ripple through her. Could she truly escape this? Could she truly break its hold?

But there was no time to dwell on uncertainty. She pushed the thought away, burying it deep. Daniel was still out there, somewhere, lost in the thrall of the Kingdom, and she wasn't leaving without him.

Her hand gripped the dagger tightly as she moved deeper into the heart of the castle. The shadows followed her like a thick mist, curling around her legs, reaching up toward her chest with clawed fingers. Every step she took felt like it was through a fog of impossible heaviness, like the castle was pressing in from all sides, its walls closing in. The pressure of it was stifling.

The corridor stretched before her, dimly lit by torches that flickered and flickered in the relentless wind. She had to force herself to keep moving forward, even though her legs felt like lead, even though the cold seemed to seep through her skin and into her very soul. It was the cold of the Kingdom, the cold of its ancient heart. She had felt it before, but never this strongly, never so close.

A sound echoed down the hall ahead of her, low and guttural, like something—someone—scraping against stone. Her breath caught in her throat as her mind raced to make sense of it. Was it Daniel? Was it another trick of the Kingdom, another manifestation of its insidious power?

"Elara..."

The voice.

But it wasn't Daniel's. The voice was deep and distorted, a rasping whisper that felt like it was coming from inside her own head. The shadows around her grew thicker, swirling as though alive, trying to claw at her, trying to draw her back.

"You can't fight me," the voice continued, growing louder with every passing second, reverberating off the stone walls. "I have always been here. You are nothing but a speck in my kingdom."

Her heart pounded in her chest, but she refused to stop. She wouldn't let fear control her—not now, not after everything she had endured. The voice could not break her resolve.

With a fierce breath, she stepped forward, forcing her legs to carry her down the dark corridor. She felt the weight of the Kingdom pressing harder against her, but her grip on the dagger tightened, her determination sharper than ever. She had to reach the heart of the castle, to find the source of this terrible power, the power that had taken Daniel and twisted him into something unrecognizable. She had to destroy it.

The corridor seemed endless, its stone walls stretching into shadow, the flickering torches casting eerie, dancing lights on the floor. She thought she saw figures in the corners of her vision—flickers of movement, like ghosts—but when she turned to look, there was nothing. The Kingdom was toying with her, testing her, trying to break her spirit before she could reach her goal.

And then, at the end of the hall, she saw it: a massive door, ornate and ancient, adorned with carvings of rainstorms and storm clouds, jagged lightning bolts stretching across the wood. The door seemed to pulse with a dark energy, a pulse that matched the beating of her own heart, a rhythm that reverberated through her very bones.

Elara took a step forward, and the door creaked open, though she hadn't touched it. The air shifted, the cold deepening, and she could feel it in her chest—the air in the room ahead was thick with power, with something dark and ancient.

She swallowed hard, her breath coming faster, her nerves on edge. This was it. This was the threshold, the point of no return. Whatever lay beyond that door would be the final test. She could feel the weight of it pressing on her, the realization that once she crossed that line, there would be no turning back. No second chances. If she failed here, if she let herself be consumed by the Kingdom, then Daniel—everything—would be lost forever.

But Elara was determined. She had come too far to falter now.

Taking a deep breath, she crossed the threshold.

The room beyond was vast, the ceiling so high it seemed to disappear into the shadows above. The stone floor was cracked, jagged, and the air was thick with the smell of damp earth and decay. The walls were lined with strange, ancient symbols—runes carved into the stone, glowing faintly, pulsing with a sickly light. And at the center of the room was something that made Elara's blood run cold: a massive, dark stone altar, dripping with water, as though it were alive. It was the source, she realized—the very heart of the Kingdom, the thing that had ensnared Daniel, that had pulled the castle into its grip.

And standing before the altar, bathed in shadow, was a figure.

Elara's heart lurched as she took in the figure before her, the person standing at the altar. The man was tall, his features hidden by the darkness, but there was something about him that seemed familiar—something about the way he stood, the way the shadows twisted around him like they were a part of him.

"Daniel?" she whispered, the word barely audible, as if speaking it too loudly would shatter the fragile illusion that this was real.

The figure didn't respond at first, but Elara could feel his eyes on her. The silence stretched between them, thick and suffocating, before he finally spoke, his voice cold and distant.

"You shouldn't have come."

The words hit her like a blow. She took a step forward, her heart leaping in her chest.

"No," she said, her voice shaking with emotion. "I'm not leaving without you."

There was a moment of stillness, the air charged with the weight of something unspeakable, and then the figure stepped into the light.

It was Daniel.

But not Daniel. His eyes were hollow, dark pools of emptiness, his face pale and drawn, the once vibrant warmth in his features now replaced by a chilling, unnatural coldness. His clothes hung off him, torn and weathered, as though he had been here, in this place, for far longer than he should have been. He was changed—marked by the Kingdom, his soul seemingly stripped away by its power.

"Elara…" His voice was softer now, almost a whisper, but there was an edge to it, a finality that sent a shiver down her spine. "It's too late. You don't understand. I made my choice. I belong here now. You can't save me."

"No!" she cried, taking another step forward. "No, Daniel. You're not gone. I won't accept it. You don't belong to this place."

The shadows around him seemed to move in response, a ripple of dark energy flowing from his body as if the Kingdom itself was reacting to her defiance.

"You can't win," he said quietly, almost sadly. "This place… it takes what it wants. And it's taken me. It's taken my soul. There's nothing left of me here, Elara. Nothing for you to save."

Her hands trembled as she raised the dagger, its blade gleaming in the dim light. She knew what she had to do. She had to destroy the heart of the Kingdom—the altar, the very source of its power. If she could destroy it, she could free him. She could free them both.

But as her hand reached for the dagger, the shadows surged around her, wrapping around her limbs, pulling her toward the altar. The voice—the Kingdom's voice—roared in her mind, filling her thoughts with doubts, with lies. The room shook violently, the very stone beneath her feet cracking, splitting.

"Elara…" Daniel's voice again, softer now, almost pleading. "Please… let go. You can't fight this. You can't fight me."

And for a moment, Elara hesitated. The darkness was so close, so strong, and she could feel it pulling her down, tempting her with the promise of release. But then she saw Daniel's eyes—the remnants of the man she loved—and in that moment, she knew what she had to do.

With every ounce of strength she could muster, she pushed through the shadows, reached deep inside herself, and drove the dagger into the stone altar.

The room exploded with light. The Kingdom screamed. And Elara felt the world shatter around her.

21

The Shattering

The world around Elara erupted in blinding light, searing her vision as though a thousand suns had risen in unison, casting everything into sharp, unyielding contrast. For a brief moment, time seemed to stop—every breath, every heartbeat held in suspended animation. The shadows recoiled, their hold on her weakening, but not disappearing entirely. The kingdom, the castle, the very air she breathed—everything seemed to convulse, like the very fabric of reality was unraveling under the weight of what she had just done.

Her hand trembled, the dagger still embedded in the stone altar, its blade glowing with a strange, pulsating energy. The light that had flooded the room now seemed to sink into the stone, like it was being absorbed, drawn into the very heart of the Kingdom. The air around her was thick, laden with a sense of finality, as though something ancient was waking, stirring, ready to claim its due.

And then, just as suddenly as the light had flared, it was gone.

The room returned to its oppressive darkness, the shadows seeping back in like water flooding through cracks. Elara's breath came in short, frantic bursts, the weight of the silence pressing down on her chest. She could feel the change in the air, the subtle shift in the atmosphere, like the entire castle was holding its breath.

"Daniel?" Her voice was barely more than a whisper, swallowed by the darkness.

For a long moment, there was nothing. Only the hollow sound of her breath, the whisper of wind seeping through cracks in the walls, the distant, eerie rumble of the storm outside. Elara stood frozen, her heart pounding in her ears, her body tense with the anticipation of something—anything—happening. She couldn't shake the feeling that the Kingdom wasn't done with her yet, that the worst was still to come.

"Elara…"

The voice, soft and familiar, cut through the silence like a blade.

Her heart leapt in her chest as she spun around, eyes wide, searching for the source of the sound. There, standing just a few feet away, was Daniel.

But not Daniel—not entirely. His form was hazy, a mirage in the dark, shifting like smoke in the dim light. He was there, and yet he wasn't. The shadows that clung to him seemed to shift and coil like living things, as though they were part of him, a part of the Kingdom he had become.

"Elara..." His voice was almost a sigh, a soft, mournful whisper that seemed to break her heart. "You shouldn't have done this."

The shadows twisted around him, wrapping tighter, pulling at him, as if the Kingdom itself were trying to pull him back. Elara's heart shattered in her chest. This wasn't the man she had fought so hard to save. This was something else—something that no longer belonged to her.

"Daniel..." she whispered, her voice breaking. "Please... I didn't want this. I didn't want to lose you."

He reached out to her, but his hand seemed to waver, his form flickering like a flame in the wind. The air around him trembled, the shadows moving with a life of their own.

"I'm sorry," he murmured, his voice barely audible, drowned out by the low rumbling of the storm outside. "I'm already gone."

Her breath caught in her throat, and she took a hesitant step toward him. "No," she whispered, shaking her head. "No, you're not gone. You're still here. I can save you. I can—"

"You can't," he interrupted, his voice sharp now, but laced with a deep, profound sadness. "The Kingdom has already taken me. There's nothing left for you to save. There's nothing left for me to give."

The shadows seemed to pulse around him, and Elara felt the air grow heavier, thicker, like the walls themselves were closing in. She could hear the Kingdom whispering to her again, the voices melding into one—low, seductive, persuasive.

"Elara..." The voice was the same as before, but this time it sounded almost... warm. "Let him go. Let it be."

"No." Elara shook her head, fighting the pull of the darkness, the lure of surrender. "I won't let you take him."

She took another step toward him, but before she could reach him, the room seemed to warp, the shadows coiling around her, tightening like chains. The floor beneath her feet cracked, a deep, jagged fissure forming along the stone, swallowing up the space between them. She stumbled back, her heart racing, fear gripping her chest.

"Please, Daniel," she cried out, her voice hoarse. "Please fight it. Fight for us. For me."

For a moment, there was silence—an unbearable, suffocating silence. Then, the shadows around Daniel seemed to shudder, as if something deep within him was struggling to break free. The darkness faltered, wavering for just a heartbeat, and Elara dared to hope.

But the hope was short-lived.

"No..." Daniel's voice came again, this time almost distant, as if it were being pulled away from her. "It's too late."

The shadows surged, pulling him back toward the altar, dragging him away from her, away from the very sliver of light that had dared to pierce the darkness. Elara tried to reach him, her legs moving instinctively, but the shadows held her fast. She couldn't move, couldn't breathe, couldn't think, as the Kingdom pulled Daniel deeper into its grip, its tendrils wrapping around him like a suffocating vine.

"Elara, listen to me," Daniel's voice broke through the storm of chaos around them, sharp and urgent. "You have to leave. You have to run. You can't save me."

"No," she screamed, her voice filled with rage and despair. "I won't leave you! I won't let the Kingdom have you!"

The shadows coiled tighter, and Elara's knees buckled, forcing her to the ground. The weight of it all was too much. The pressure, the darkness, the storm—it was all pressing in on her, suffocating her, threatening to swallow her whole.

The air grew thick with the pulse of the Kingdom, as if it were alive, as if it were feeding on her fear, on her sorrow. The walls trembled again, the very foundation of the castle groaning as if it were in agony.

"You don't understand," Daniel's voice was barely more than a whisper now, distant and lost. "The Kingdom wants me. It wants all of me. There's nothing left for you here."

The shadows around him pulsed, thickening, consuming him piece by piece. And with that, a terrible realization hit Elara.

He was right.

The Kingdom wasn't just a place—it was a force, a living entity, and it wasn't going to let either of them go. She had thought that by destroying the altar, by shattering its power, she could save him. But in truth, she had only made things worse.

Her chest tightened as she realized the cost of what she had done. The altar was gone, the heart of the Kingdom shattered, but in its wake, something else had awakened—something far darker, far more powerful than she had ever imagined.

And now, it was taking Daniel. Bit by bit, piece by piece.

"Please…" Elara whispered, her voice breaking with raw emotion. "Don't go."

But the shadows continued to drag him away, his form flickering, becoming more ethereal with each passing second. Her heart shattered, the weight of her failure crashing down on her like a wave. She had failed. She had failed him. And there was nothing she could do to stop it.

As the last remnants of Daniel vanished into the darkness, a single, mournful cry echoed through the castle, reverberating against the walls, against the storm. And for a moment, just a fleeting moment, Elara thought she heard his voice—faint, far off, but unmistakable.

"Elara…"

And then, silence.

The Kingdom had taken him.

The darkness closed in around her, swallowing the room, swallowing everything.

And Elara was left standing alone in the heart of the storm.

22

The Final Choice

The air was thick with the scent of damp stone and decaying wood. The sound of the storm outside seemed distant now, muted by the heavy silence that enveloped the room. Elara's breath came in shallow gasps, each exhale a cloud of mist in the cold air. The dark shadows, once swirling around her like a living thing, had now settled, clinging to the walls like old memories. The castle, the Kingdom—it felt more like a tomb now than the living, breathing place it had once been.

Her heart was still racing, her mind reeling from the sudden shift. Daniel was gone, lost to the shadows, to the Kingdom that had claimed him. And yet, even in the depths of her grief, a spark of defiance remained, a tiny flame that refused to be snuffed out.

"Elara…"

The voice came again, faint and distant, just a whisper in the cold. Her heart lurched in her chest. It wasn't Daniel—this time, she was certain of it. This voice, this presence—it was different. It was darker, more insistent.

She turned sharply, her eyes scanning the dim, oppressive space. Her hand gripped the hilt of the dagger still clutched tightly in her palm, the blade warm with the remnants of the altar's magic. The dagger was the only thing that remained of her defiance, her hope—everything else had been consumed by the Kingdom's relentless pull.

"Elara..."

The voice again. Closer this time.

She spun around, the shadows around her shifting, coiling like snakes. Her pulse quickened, and she could feel a bead of sweat slip down the back of her neck. She wasn't alone. The Kingdom was watching her, waiting for her to make her next move.

"Elara, you cannot escape."

The voice came from the far corner of the room, and though the words were spoken softly, they held an undeniable power—an authority that made her skin crawl. She knew, deep down, that this was not a voice she could ignore. It was the Kingdom's voice—the voice of the force that had trapped them all, that had consumed everything in its path.

She stepped backward, her feet moving almost instinctively, but the shadows pressed in closer, the walls of the room seeming to close around her with every step she took.

"You've made a grave mistake," the voice continued, each word heavy with a promise of consequence. "You should have left when you had the chance. You should have surrendered."

Elara's eyes darted to the door, the only escape she could see, but it was no longer there. The walls had closed off every exit, leaving her trapped in this suffocating room with whatever it was that had been waiting for her. The air seemed to grow colder, sharper, as if the room itself were taking a deep, suffocating breath.

"You thought you could save him," the voice mocked, a strange, hollow laugh echoing in the space around her. "But you were always meant to fail. The Kingdom does not let go. It does not forgive."

Her grip on the dagger tightened. "I don't care," she whispered through clenched teeth. "I don't care what the Kingdom does. I'll fight until my last breath."

A low rumble vibrated through the floor beneath her feet. The shadows surged, as though reacting to her words, and the temperature in the room seemed to drop further, seeping into her bones. The dagger in her hand hummed with a strange energy, as if the Kingdom itself was trying to claim it, to twist it to its will.

"Elara, Elara…" The voice was softer now, almost soothing. "Why fight against what you are?"

She froze, the words sinking into her like a weight. There was something familiar about the voice, something... unsettling. It seemed to know her, to know her thoughts, her fears, her darkest desires.

"You've always known, haven't you?" it said, a strange warmth creeping into the coldness of the room. "You were always meant for this. You were always meant to be part of this."

The shadows shifted again, a shape taking form in the corner of the room, a silhouette that seemed to emerge from the darkness itself. It was a figure—tall, imposing, cloaked in a robe of midnight black. Elara's heart skipped a beat as the figure stepped into the dim light, its face hidden beneath a hood, but she could feel the eyes upon her, the weight of them, pressing against her like a physical force.

"Elara," the figure spoke again, its voice more familiar now. "I am the Kingdom. I am its heart, its soul. And you... you are a part of me."

The words hit her like a physical blow. Her breath caught in her throat as the realization began to settle in—slow, cold, and awful. The figure before her wasn't just a manifestation of the Kingdom. It wasn't some ancient, distant force. It was something more.

It was her.

No, not her. Not exactly.

But it was the truth, and it was undeniable. There was a

connection—an intimate, undeniable bond between Elara and the Kingdom. She had felt it since the moment she had first set foot in this place. The whispers, the strange sense of familiarity, the pull of the shadows. The Kingdom had never just been a prison. It had been inside her all along.

"Elara," the figure repeated, its voice like silk, like the temptation of a dream. "You've always known you were meant for this. For me. You were born of the Kingdom, born of its rain, of its storm. You can't escape it, not anymore. You are part of its blood."

She shook her head violently, backing away. "No. I am not you. I will never be you."

The figure stepped forward, its hood falling back to reveal a face—her face. Her own features, twisted, pale, and shadowed, stared back at her, an impossible reflection. The eyes were hollow, drained of any warmth, any light. The face was both familiar and foreign, a sickening reflection of herself.

The figure smiled, and the smile was all darkness. "You cannot escape your nature, Elara. You can fight it, you can struggle, but in the end, you will always return to me. The Kingdom and I are one. And you... you are the key to its rebirth."

Elara stumbled backward, her knees giving out beneath her as the weight of the revelation crashed down on her. The room tilted, the walls seeming to shift, swirl like water around her. The dagger in her hand felt heavy, its power now foreign to her, as if it no longer belonged in her grip.

"No," she whispered, the word torn from her lips, as though her very soul was trying to deny what she was seeing. "No, I am not you. I won't be part of this."

The figure reached out, its hand cold and unfeeling as it brushed against her cheek. "You already are," it said softly, its voice a caress, a whisper that seemed to seep into her very skin. "You've always been part of it. All you have to do is accept it. All you have to do is surrender."

Her breath hitched as she tried to push away from the figure, but it was no use. The shadows around her closed in, pulling her back, wrapping around her legs, her arms, her throat. The Kingdom's pulse seemed to resonate inside her chest, matching her heartbeat, echoing in her mind.

"Elara, you are mine," the figure said, its voice growing more insistent, more forceful. "You were born of the rain, of the storm. You are the storm. And now you will bring it."

She closed her eyes, shaking her head in disbelief, in denial, in fear. The air around her thickened, her chest tightening as though the very walls of the castle were pressing against her, suffocating her, demanding her surrender.

But in that moment, as the shadows closed in, something inside her shifted. Something deep, something ancient, awakened within her—the storm that had always been a part of her, the part that had been calling out from within. And in that moment, as the Kingdom reached out to claim her, she realized what she had to do.

THE FINAL CHOICE

She had a choice.

She could surrender—allow herself to be consumed, allow the Kingdom to take its rightful place, to absorb her into its dark heart. Or she could fight.

Elara's grip tightened around the dagger. The weight of the choice, the weight of the power inside her, pulsed against her skin. She felt the Kingdom's heart beating through her, the storm inside her rising.

She made her choice.

With a cry of defiance, Elara drove the dagger into her own chest.

23

The Heart of the Storm

The moment the dagger pierced her skin, time seemed to fracture. The world around her spun and twisted like a tempest unleashed, every breath a struggle against the weight of her own choice. Elara's vision blurred, a strange fog settling over her thoughts as the power of the Kingdom surged through her veins. The darkness that had once seemed so distant, so foreign, now felt like a part of her, alive and pulsing within her chest.

The air around her thickened, growing heavy with the promise of something unimaginable. The shadows that clung to the walls stretched toward her, their forms writhing, their whispers louder now, filling her mind with a cacophony of voices, each more insistent than the last. It was as though the Kingdom itself were speaking directly to her, claiming her, pulling her into its depths.

But Elara held on. Despite the pain, despite the darkness that sought to consume her, she clung to the flame of defiance burning within her. The Kingdom had thought it could break her. It had thought it could make her one of its own. But the truth was far simpler, far more dangerous. She wasn't meant to be the Kingdom's queen. She wasn't meant to be its puppet.

She was meant to destroy it.

With every pulse of her heart, every beat of her blood, she could feel the power of the storm gathering. The Kingdom was a living thing, yes—but it was a thing built on lies, built on broken promises and shattered souls. And Elara was no longer a part of its designs. She had severed the tie.

The shadows around her trembled, their whispers turning frantic, as though they could sense the shift, as though they could feel the change within her. They pressed in closer, curling around her like serpents ready to strike, their cold tendrils reaching for her, eager to drag her back into the depths. But Elara wasn't afraid. She wasn't afraid anymore.

"Elara..."

The voice came again, a low murmur that sent a shiver down her spine. It was familiar—too familiar. Her eyes snapped open, and she saw the figure standing before her. It was Daniel—or at least, it looked like him. His form was hazy, shifting in and out of focus like a mirage in the storm.

"Elara, you can't do this," Daniel's voice cracked, a raw pleading edge creeping into the words. "This isn't the way. The Kingdom will destroy you."

She felt the pull of his words, the weight of his sorrow, but she didn't move. She couldn't. She couldn't give in to the doubt creeping into her chest, the fear gnawing at the edges of her resolve. She had made her choice, and no matter how it hurt, no matter what it cost her, she wasn't going to turn back.

"I'm not afraid of the Kingdom anymore," she said, her voice firm, despite the tremor in her limbs. "I'm not afraid of anything."

For a long moment, there was silence. Daniel's form flickered, his face filled with a mixture of pain and understanding, as though he knew, deep down, what she was about to do. But the shadows—the Kingdom—were relentless, and they weren't done with her yet.

The room began to shift again, the walls warping and bending as if the very fabric of reality was bending to the will of the Kingdom. The ground beneath her feet trembled, the stones cracking with the force of something vast, something ancient stirring deep within the castle's foundation.

"Elara..." The voice came again, this time clearer, more commanding. The figure of Daniel began to fade, replaced by something darker, something more powerful. The air around her grew thick with an oppressive weight, and the shadows writhed and twisted, becoming something far more dangerous than she had ever imagined.

It wasn't just the Kingdom speaking to her anymore. It was the heart of the Kingdom, the thing that had been pulling the strings all along, the force that had bound her to this place from the very beginning.

"You are mine," the voice echoed, its words resounding through her mind, through the very marrow of her bones. "You cannot escape me."

She could feel the storm inside her rising, the power of the Kingdom clashing with the defiance that had taken root in her heart. The dagger in her chest burned, its power now both her weapon and her curse. She could feel the Kingdom's grip tightening, trying to claim her, trying to make her part of its dark heart.

But she wouldn't let it. She wouldn't give in.

With a cry of determination, Elara pulled the dagger from her chest, the blade slick with her blood. She held it before her, her fingers trembling around the hilt, and with every ounce of strength she had left, she thrust the blade forward, slashing through the air with a force she didn't know she possessed.

The room shook as though struck by a thunderclap. The air cracked with the sound of breaking glass, of tearing fabric, of something ancient and powerful snapping in two.

For a moment, the world stood still. The shadows paused, the storm outside stilled, and for the briefest instant, Elara felt the heavy weight of the Kingdom's hold loosen. The pulse of its power faded, like the last flicker of a dying flame. She was free.

But then the darkness surged again, this time more furious, more desperate. The storm within her raged, and she could feel the Kingdom fighting back, its tendrils curling tighter around her, pulling her into its depths.

"No," she whispered, gritting her teeth against the pain, against the overwhelming force threatening to crush her. "I won't be yours."

Her voice rang out, clear and defiant, as she drove the dagger into the ground, plunging it deep into the stone. The room trembled violently, the air thickening with an overwhelming pressure, as though the very walls of the castle were groaning under the weight of her will.

And then, the Kingdom roared.

It was a sound that shook her to her core, a deep, guttural cry that filled the room and echoed through the entire castle, as if the very stones of the castle were alive with fury. The shadows surged forward, crashing against her like a tidal wave, but Elara stood her ground, her feet planted firmly on the ground.

The storm inside her flared, wild and untamed, and she could feel the heart of the Kingdom—its true heart—beating beneath her feet, pulsing with dark energy. It was a living thing, a force that thrived on power and fear. It would never let her go, not unless she made it.

"Elara..."

The voice again, but this time, it wasn't Daniel. It wasn't even the Kingdom speaking to her. It was something else, something deeper, something far older.

She felt the cold, ancient power rise within her, a force that connected her to the very heart of the storm. Her blood pulsed with the energy of the Kingdom, but it was her blood now—her storm, her fight.

With a cry that split the air, Elara raised the dagger high, and in a single, powerful strike, she drove it deep into the stone of the castle floor.

The ground shattered.

The world trembled.

And the storm exploded.

It was as though the very foundation of the Kingdom had been torn asunder. The walls cracked and crumbled, the air crackling with energy, with power beyond her comprehension. The shadows screamed, a sound like the wailing of a thousand lost souls, but Elara stood firm, her grip on the dagger unwavering. The storm inside her surged, filling her with a strength she had never known, a power that shattered the very darkness that had sought to control her.

And as the Kingdom's heart cracked, as its power faltered and broke, Elara felt the storm inside her fade. The shadows disappeared, the walls stopped shaking, and the air cleared.

The castle was still.

But she wasn't alone.

Standing before her, his form flickering in the remnants of the storm's energy, was Daniel. His face was bruised, his eyes wide, but alive.

"Elara," he whispered, his voice weak but filled with relief. "You did it."

She stumbled forward, collapsing into his arms, the weight of everything finally catching up to her. The storm inside her faded, leaving only the quiet echo of its power. And for the first time in a long while, Elara let herself breathe, the storm's final roar fading into nothingness.

They were free.

But Elara knew the cost. The Kingdom had been torn apart, but it was not gone. Not entirely. Its heart had shattered, but something remained. A whisper. A threat.

She didn't know what would come next.

But for now, in that fragile moment of peace, she allowed herself to believe that maybe, just maybe, they had won.

24

The Aftermath of Silence

The storm had passed.

Elara sat in the center of the crumbling castle, her body aching and her mind still spinning from the chaos of the battle. Her hands were covered in blood—hers, his, the Kingdom's—but she barely noticed it anymore. The air around her was thick with the weight of the silence. There was no wind, no thunder, no crackling energy in the atmosphere. The Kingdom's pulse had stopped.

But she could still feel the remnants of it, the strange echo reverberating through the ruins of the castle. It was as if the very walls were holding their breath, waiting for something, anything, to break the stillness.

Daniel had fallen beside her, too exhausted to stand, but too relieved to say anything. They had fought through the heart of the storm together, and now that it was over, there was nothing left to do but breathe. Neither of them spoke, neither of them moved, as the hours stretched out in oppressive stillness.

"Elara..."

Her heart skipped a beat at the sound of his voice. It was quiet, fragile, as though he, too, feared breaking the silence.

She turned toward him. His face was pale, drawn with exhaustion, but his eyes were alive. The light had returned to them. The shadows that had once claimed him were gone, vanished like smoke in the wind. She reached out for him instinctively, her fingers trembling as they brushed against his arm.

"We did it," he whispered, as though he couldn't quite believe the words. "We actually did it."

But Elara didn't answer. She was staring past him, her gaze fixed on the ruins of the Kingdom that lay scattered around them. The once-majestic halls, the chambers that had held so many secrets, now lay in ruins. The walls were cracked, the stained-glass windows shattered. The throne, the symbol of the Kingdom's power, had fallen, its golden frame twisted and broken beneath the weight of the storm.

The world around them was still. Too still.

It felt wrong.

"Elara, are you... are you okay?" Daniel's voice was full of concern now, his hand reaching out to touch hers, pulling her from her thoughts.

She looked at him, forcing a small smile. "I'm fine," she said, though the words felt hollow. She wasn't fine. Not at all.

Something was still lingering, something she couldn't shake off. The storm had been defeated, the heart of the Kingdom shattered, but there was a sense of unease gnawing at her—a cold, creeping feeling that told her this wasn't over. Not by a long shot.

"Elara..." Daniel started again, his voice faltering this time, but she raised a hand to stop him. She couldn't listen to him right now. She couldn't bear to hear any more reassurances, not when everything inside her was screaming that they hadn't finished their work.

"Do you hear that?" she asked softly, her voice barely above a whisper.

Daniel froze, his hand still on hers. His eyes darted around the room, his body tensing, but he shook his head. "Hear what?"

"The silence," Elara said, her voice hardening. "It's too quiet. It shouldn't be like this."

Her words hung in the air, and for a moment, she thought she might be imagining it, that perhaps the darkness of the Kingdom had left a scar on her mind, a lingering shadow. But then she felt it again, that pull—faint but undeniable—a sensation deep in the pit of her stomach. It was a feeling she knew all too well.

The Kingdom wasn't gone. It was just... hiding.

"Elara..." Daniel's voice cracked, his fingers squeezing hers. "Please, don't. You're just tired. We're free. We can—"

"No, Daniel." Her voice was sharp, cutting through his words like a blade. "We haven't finished this. The Kingdom doesn't just... disappear. It doesn't let go that easily."

A tense silence fell between them, both of them acutely aware of the truth in her words. Elara stood up slowly, her legs weak, but her resolve as firm as it had ever been. She ignored the dizziness threatening to overwhelm her, focusing instead on the broken walls, the shattered windows, the quiet that had become so deafening.

"There's something wrong," she muttered under her breath. "I can feel it."

Daniel stood, hesitantly at first, then more firmly as if trying to reassure himself, though the doubt was written all over his face. "What are you saying? That it's still here? After everything?"

"I don't know," Elara said, glancing around the darkened room. "But I have a feeling. We've only just begun to unravel it. The Kingdom may have crumbled, but its essence—its power—it's still lingering."

She moved forward, each step deliberate, each movement more confident than the last. She couldn't explain it. She couldn't pinpoint it, but something was alive within the castle's bones—

something far older than the Kingdom itself.

And then she heard it.

A low, guttural growl.

It came from deep within the castle, from somewhere below them, from the very heart of the ruins. The sound reverberated through the stone, shaking the floor beneath their feet.

"Elara," Daniel said, his voice barely above a whisper. "What is that?"

"I don't know," she said, her heart pounding, but she didn't hesitate. The dagger was still in her hand, its blade stained with the remnants of the storm. She gripped it tighter and started walking toward the source of the noise, her steps sure, even though her mind screamed at her to turn back.

"Elara, wait!" Daniel called after her, but she didn't stop.

She reached the central hall, and the growling intensified, a low, primal sound that seemed to shake the very foundation of the castle. The air was thick with heat now, a strange, oppressive warmth that had no place in the cold ruins. It was as if something was waking up, something ancient, something far more dangerous than the Kingdom itself.

Her pulse quickened as she descended the spiraling staircase into the lower chambers. The walls were dark, covered in mildew and creeping vines, but the strange warmth was still there, growing stronger with every step. She could feel it in her chest, the thrum of power pulsing beneath her skin. She could feel its call.

"Elara, stop!" Daniel's voice was strained now, frantic. "This is madness. It's gone. The Kingdom is—"

"No," Elara interrupted, her voice low and tight. "It's not gone. It's still here. I can feel it."

She reached the bottom of the stairs and found herself in the heart of the castle's oldest chambers. The air was thick, heavy with the scent of rot and decay. The flickering shadows seemed to move on their own, twisting like serpents, and the temperature dropped again, the warmth vanishing as quickly as it had appeared.

The growling had stopped.

For a moment, there was silence again, but it wasn't the same as before. This silence was different. It was the calm before the storm. The silence of something waiting.

And then, Elara saw it.

A shadow, darker than anything she had ever seen, larger than any human form, emerged from the far corner of the chamber. It moved slowly, its shape shifting, its body fluid and liquid, like a creature made of smoke and shadows. It was enormous, its presence filling the space, suffocating the air.

Elara didn't move. Her fingers tightened around the dagger, and she took a step forward, her heart racing. She could feel the weight of its gaze on her, the power of it pressing in on her from all sides.

It spoke, but its voice was like nothing she had ever heard before—low, ancient, and impossibly cold.

"Elara..."

Her breath caught in her throat. This wasn't the Kingdom's voice, not completely. It was something more. Something worse.

"You... thought you could destroy me," it hissed. "But you don't understand. I am not bound by your rules, your magic, your destiny. I am the heart of all things."

Elara's knees weakened, her pulse racing as the shadows pressed closer. But she stood firm. She wouldn't be afraid. She couldn't afford to be.

"You're wrong," she said, her voice steady despite the fear coiling in her chest. "I've destroyed you before. I can do it again."

The shadow shrieked, an unearthly sound that made the very stone around them vibrate. "You think you've won?" it laughed, its voice echoing through the chamber. "You have merely unleashed the true power of the Kingdom."

Elara's eyes narrowed. She wasn't going to let this thing take her again. It had consumed too many lives already—Daniel's, her own. She would not allow it to claim another.

With all the strength she had left, she lunged forward, the dagger raised high.

And this time, there would be no hesitation. No fear. Only the storm.

25

Into the Abyss

The darkness around Elara thickened, curling in on itself like a vast, suffocating void. She felt the air grow colder with every step she took toward the shadow, the thing that had once been the Kingdom's heart, now alive in ways she couldn't begin to comprehend. Her fingers clenched around the hilt of the dagger, the cold steel pressing against her palm, grounding her even as her body trembled from the sheer weight of what was happening. The shadow before her was not like anything she had ever encountered—it was ancient, unfathomable, a force far older than the Kingdom itself.

And yet, it was familiar.

She could feel it inside her, like a pulse within her blood, thrumming in sync with her heart. This was the Kingdom's true essence, the core from which its power had radiated. All along, it had been manipulating, controlling, waiting for someone to awaken it fully. And Elara had done just that.

With every breath, the room seemed to grow darker, the space around her warping as the shadow stretched impossibly tall, its form shifting in unnatural ways, as though it existed in a thousand different dimensions at once. It was a thing of nightmares, a terror woven from the fabric of time itself.

"Elara…" The voice came again, deeper this time, reverberating through the very stone beneath her feet. "You've come too far, child. You've awakened me, and now you cannot undo what's been done."

She stood motionless, the dagger raised before her, its blade gleaming faintly in the dim light of the chamber. The figure before her was more than just a shadow—it was a manifestation of everything the Kingdom had ever been. All its dark power, its manipulation, its insidious control over the land and its people—it was all contained within this monstrous being, this ancient force that sought to consume all that dared challenge it.

But Elara wasn't afraid.

Not anymore.

"I don't have to undo anything," she said, her voice calm, despite the pounding of her heart. "You were never meant to be. I'm here to end this. To destroy you once and for all."

The shadow laughed, its voice like a thousand broken echoes, distorting the air around them. It was a sound that seemed to tear at the very fabric of reality, twisting the world in painful ways. "Destroy me? You think you have the power to do that? You think you can rid the world of me?"

Elara's grip tightened around the dagger. She could feel the tremor of the storm still lingering in her chest, the remnants of its power crackling along her skin. It had been quiet for so long, but now it surged again, a restless force yearning to be unleashed.

She had felt its pull—the Kingdom's essence—before, in the deepest recesses of her soul. It had always been there, lurking, waiting for her to discover it, to embrace it. And now, in this moment, as the shadow before her towered like an insurmountable mountain, she understood the truth: The Kingdom had never been a place. It had never been a kingdom of people, of land, or even of power. It had been a parasite, a presence, living in the hearts of those who dared to think they could control it.

And she had become its undoing.

"Your time is over," she said, her voice now unwavering, filled with the strength that had been forged through every trial, every loss, and every victory.

The shadow seemed to recoil at her words, its form flickering, but it quickly regained its shape, its presence even more overwhelming than before. "You don't understand," it hissed, its voice like nails scraping across stone. "I am everything. I am the darkness that birthed this world, the force that drives it forward. Without me, there is nothing. You are nothing."

"No," Elara replied, her voice steady. "I am everything. I am the one who chose to fight, the one who defied you. I am the storm that will wipe you away."

Her words seemed to cut through the air, each syllable slicing through the tension like a blade. She could feel the power of the storm—the true storm—gathering within her, coursing through her veins, twisting around her heart. It wasn't the Kingdom's storm anymore. It was hers.

And in that moment, Elara understood. This wasn't just a battle against the Kingdom. It wasn't just about power or control. It was about choice. It was about her will, her desire to forge her own path, to reclaim what had been stolen from her.

The shadow lunged at her, its dark tendrils reaching out like grasping hands, but Elara didn't flinch. She had fought too hard to be afraid now. With a primal scream, she raised the dagger high, plunging it deep into the floor. The ground beneath her feet cracked open, a massive shockwave rippling outward as the power within her surged.

The shadow recoiled again, its form beginning to fracture, but Elara could feel the resistance. The force that had held it together, the remnants of the Kingdom's soul, were powerful. It was an ancient magic, one that couldn't be undone so easily. But she wasn't backing down.

"Elara..." The shadow's voice trembled, growing weaker with every passing second. It was no longer the voice of the Kingdom, but the voice of desperation. "You can't win. You can't fight me forever."

Elara didn't respond. Instead, she focused all her energy on the storm within her, letting it fill every inch of her being. The darkness that had once sought to consume her was now her weapon, her strength. She had learned to control it, to bend it to her will.

And now, she would use it to destroy everything it had created.

With a final, decisive movement, she thrust the dagger forward, the blade glowing with an eerie light. The shadow shrieked as the blade pierced its core, its form beginning to disintegrate, its essence unraveling like smoke in the wind. The darkness twisted and writhed, but it was no match for the power Elara now wielded.

The storm inside her roared to life, its fury unleashed, its energy surging outward in a blinding explosion of light. The ground beneath her feet trembled violently, cracks forming in the stone as the very foundations of the castle began to crumble. The castle shook, its walls disintegrating, its ruins falling apart piece by piece.

And yet, Elara stood firm, her heart steady, her mind clear.

The shadow screamed once more, its voice now a broken, fragmented sound, and with a final surge of power, it dissipated entirely, vanishing into the air, leaving nothing behind but the remnants of its dark presence.

For a moment, everything was silent. The storm within her had faded, the power that had once surged so violently now dissipating like a storm that had passed. The air was still, the oppressive weight of the darkness now lifted.

But Elara knew that the battle wasn't truly over.

The castle had fallen, the heart of the Kingdom had been destroyed, but there was still the matter of what remained—of what had been left in the wake of its destruction.

Daniel's voice broke the silence. "Elara…"

She turned to face him, her heart still racing, her body still trembling from the sheer force of what had just transpired. He stood at the entrance to the chamber, his face pale but filled with relief. But his eyes—they were filled with something else now. Something that made her hesitate.

"What happens now?" he asked, his voice tentative, unsure.

Elara looked around her, taking in the ruin, the destruction, the emptiness that now filled the space. The shadow was gone, but the air still seemed heavy, as though it was holding its breath. She had won the battle, but the war—whatever war had started with the rise of the Kingdom—was far from over.

"I don't know," she whispered, her voice distant. "But I won't stop. Not now. Not after everything we've lost."

The castle groaned, its foundation shifting once again, as if in response to her words. Elara didn't flinch. She knew this place was collapsing, its dark heart no longer able to sustain it. The Kingdom had been a house of cards, and she had torn it down.

But even now, she could feel the remnants of its power—the faintest stirrings of something ancient, something that still sought to rise.

"Elara..." Daniel's voice cut through her thoughts again. "What are we going to do?"

She turned to him, her expression hardening, her eyes filled with a quiet determination.

"We fight," she said softly, her gaze turning toward the ruins, the broken kingdom, and the future that still awaited them. "We rebuild. And we make sure that nothing like this ever rises again."

26

The Last Whisper

The sky above was a patchwork of gray and bruised purple as the remnants of the storm finally began to fade. The once-foreboding clouds seemed to part reluctantly, the last vestiges of the tempest dissipating like smoke caught in a gentle breeze. Beneath the vast expanse of the heavens, the kingdom lay in ruin—its heart broken, its soul scattered to the winds, and yet... the air still felt thick with something unseen, something waiting.

Elara stood at the edge of what had once been the royal courtyard, her body bruised and battered, but her resolve unbroken. The dagger that had ended the nightmare—ended the Kingdom—still hung loosely from her hand. The blade had been forged with blood and fire, and now, it felt cold and heavy, as though it, too, understood the weight of what had just transpired.

Beside her, Daniel remained quiet, his face a mask of exhaustion and disbelief. He had seen it all—the storm, the shadow,

Elara's unflinching determination to fight. And yet, even as they stood together in the aftermath, a lingering sense of dread gnawed at the edges of his mind, as though something was still lurking just beyond the horizon, waiting to resurface.

"I can't believe it's over," he said finally, his voice hoarse from the battle and the dust that clung to the air. "It feels... wrong, somehow."

Elara didn't respond at first. Instead, her gaze remained fixed on the horizon, on the distant mountains that loomed like silent sentinels in the twilight. The sun was setting now, casting long shadows over the kingdom's broken spires and shattered walls. There was something in the silence—the stillness—that made the weight of the moment feel even more oppressive. It was as if the earth itself was holding its breath.

"I know," she said softly, her voice barely above a whisper. "It feels like a dream. Like we haven't really won... not yet."

Daniel's brow furrowed as he turned toward her, concern flashing in his eyes. "What do you mean? We've destroyed the Kingdom. The storm is gone. The shadow is gone. Everything should be... finished."

Elara shook her head slowly, her fingers gripping the dagger's hilt tighter. "It's not over. Not entirely. We've broken the Kingdom, but its essence... its influence is still out there. It's in the air, Daniel. It's in the land. And as long as it remains, there will always be a chance for it to return."

Daniel opened his mouth to protest, but something in her expression silenced him. He had seen the fire in her eyes, had felt the storm raging within her every time she faced down their enemies, but now there was something else—a quiet certainty that unsettled him more than any battle had.

"Elara, we've lost so much. We've fought and bled for this moment. Can't we just... rest?" His voice cracked with the weight of his exhaustion. "Can't we just rebuild, find some peace?"

Elara turned to face him fully now, her gaze softening. She placed a hand gently on his arm, feeling the tremble in his muscles as he fought to keep himself steady. "I want peace, Daniel. I do. But peace isn't given to us. It's something we have to create. Something we have to protect."

She stepped away from him, her eyes scanning the broken kingdom before them. The walls were nothing more than jagged remnants of what had once been—a reflection of the battle they had fought and won, but also a reminder of the cost. What remained was a fractured shell of a kingdom that had been built on lies and blood.

"I'll never stop fighting," Elara said quietly, more to herself than to Daniel. "Not until the last of its influence is gone. Until this land is truly free."

There was a silence between them then, a long, heavy pause as Daniel absorbed her words. He watched her, his gaze tracing the subtle lines of determination etched into her face, the faint tremor in her hand that told him how deeply the battle had affected her. She wasn't just fighting for herself anymore. She was fighting for everyone. For the land, for the people, for everything that had been crushed under the Kingdom's rule.

"I understand," he said finally, his voice barely above a whisper. "I'll fight, too. Until the very end."

Elara nodded, a flicker of something—relief? Gratitude?—passing across her face. She didn't want to be alone in this fight, and though she had always carried the burden of the Kingdom's destruction on her shoulders, she knew she wasn't alone now.

The moment was brief, but in it, Elara could feel the remnants of the storm—the tension, the doubt, the fear—finally begin to lift. They had faced the Kingdom's darkest force, had survived its most vicious storm, and together, they had shattered it. But there was more to be done.

The battle hadn't been won just by breaking the Kingdom's heart. That had only been the first step. The true war would be the one to follow.

And as she stood there, with the sky fading into the bruised hues of twilight, Elara realized the full scope of what lay ahead. The shadow had been a parasite, a force that had clung to the land, twisted its people, and seeped into every corner of the world. The Kingdom's fall had been the first chapter, but now, Elara knew, they were about to face the hardest part: the rebuilding.

"We'll start small," Elara murmured, more to herself than to Daniel. "We'll rebuild the people, one by one. We'll remind them of the world before the Kingdom. The world before the darkness. We'll remind them that they are free."

Daniel stepped forward, his expression resolute. "And how do we do that?"

Elara smiled faintly, her eyes lighting with a quiet fire. "We give them hope. We show them that it's not too late to start again."

For a moment, there was nothing but the distant sound of wind rustling through the trees, the soft whisper of the world beginning to heal. And then, as if in response to her words, a gust of wind swept through the courtyard, brushing against Elara's skin like a fleeting caress.

"Elara..." Daniel's voice was strained now, his eyes narrowing in concern. "What's that?"

Elara's heart skipped a beat. The air had shifted. She could feel it again—the presence that had lingered since the storm. It was faint, but undeniable. A whisper, just on the edge of her senses, like a breath on the wind.

She turned quickly, her instincts flaring. It was coming from the castle ruins, from deep within the broken halls, where the shadows were thickest. There was something there. Something waiting.

"Stay here," she ordered, her voice low and tense, her hand reaching instinctively for the dagger. But as she moved toward the ruins, Daniel caught her arm.

"Elara, no," he said urgently. "Don't. You can't keep doing this. It's over."

She shook her head, her eyes flashing. "You don't understand. It's never over. Not while there's even the smallest trace of it left."

Elara stepped away, her heart pounding in her chest as she moved toward the ruins. With every step, the air grew heavier, colder, and the whispering grew louder, more distinct, as though it was speaking directly to her. The language was strange, ancient, filled with echoes of a time long past.

It was the Kingdom's voice.

Her hand trembled as she reached the broken archway, the remnants of the castle's once-grand entrance standing like a hollow monument to what had been lost. There, among the ruins, a figure stood—tall, dark, and cloaked in shadows.

"Elara…" the figure whispered, its voice smooth and deadly.

Elara froze, her pulse quickening. She knew this voice. She had heard it before, in her dreams, in her nightmares.

It was him.

The true source of the Kingdom's power.

"Elara, you thought you had destroyed me," the figure said, stepping forward. His face remained shrouded in darkness, but his voice was unmistakable. "But you were wrong. I am not a kingdom, Elara. I am the storm."

And with that, the whispering grew into a deafening roar, and Elara's world shattered once again.

27

The Storm's Return

Elara's breath hitched, her entire body going rigid as the shadowed figure before her stepped into the faint light that flickered through the ruins of the castle. His form seemed to shimmer, the edges of his cloak merging with the air around him like smoke drifting in the wind. The voice—the same voice that had once whispered promises of dominion and control—was now thick with an unmistakable threat.

"I'm not just the storm, Elara," he said, his voice low, resonating deep in her chest. "I am the storm. I am the heartbeat of the Kingdom—the force that binds this world together and tears it apart. And you, foolish girl, thought you could destroy me."

The words twisted in her mind, the truth of them sinking into her like cold, sharp steel. It had been him all along— the true force behind the Kingdom, behind the shadow that had corrupted everything she had fought to protect. She had thought the battle was over. She had thought the storm had been quelled, the darkness vanquished.

But this? This was something worse.

Her pulse quickened, and she instinctively reached for the dagger at her side. The blade had been forged for this purpose, for this final act of defiance, but now, it felt almost insignificant against the overwhelming power before her. The figure, tall and ethereal, was like a force of nature—a living embodiment of everything the Kingdom had stood for, of everything Elara had tried to destroy.

"You thought you could end it," he continued, stepping closer. His eyes—deep, hollow voids that seemed to pierce through the very fabric of her being—locked onto hers with an intensity that made her skin crawl. "But the Kingdom doesn't die, Elara. It cannot. It will always return, for it is a part of this world, as I am. You have only delayed the inevitable."

Elara's heart hammered in her chest, but she didn't back away. She could feel the storm within her, the lingering remnants of the power she had tapped into earlier, but it was faint now—just a flicker of the force it had been. The storm had been a part of her, too. She had been consumed by it, controlled by it. But now, it was as though that bond had been severed, leaving her weak, exposed, and vulnerable.

She tightened her grip on the dagger, her mind racing. The figure before her wasn't just a man or a shadow; he was the storm, the embodiment of the very chaos that had plagued the Kingdom. And now, he had returned, stronger than ever.

"You were never meant to destroy me, Elara," he said, his voice a soft, mocking lilt. "You were meant to free me."

"Free you?" Elara spat, her voice trembling with fury. "You think I'd ever free you? You destroyed everything I loved. You destroyed my family, my home, my people. I fought for this world, for a chance to rebuild it, and now—now you think I'll let you win?"

The figure's lips curled into a smile that didn't reach his eyes, an expression that sent a shiver down her spine. "You think this is a fight? This is destiny, Elara. You cannot change what is meant to be. The Kingdom will rise again, and you will be the one to lead it."

The words sank in like poison, twisting her insides. Lead the Kingdom? She had fought to destroy it, to break free from its suffocating grip, and now he wanted her to lead it? To be a part of the very thing that had ruined her life?

"I'll never lead you," Elara said, her voice a low, dangerous whisper. "I will end this. You are nothing. You are just a shadow, a relic of a past that should have never existed."

The figure laughed, a deep, rumbling sound that reverberated through the air. It was a laugh full of ancient knowledge, full of power that Elara could barely comprehend. It made her feel small, insignificant—like a mere speck in the grand scheme of things.

"You think you can end me?" he asked, his voice dripping with disdain. "You cannot end what you do not understand, Elara.

You are the storm. You always have been."

The words hit her like a blow to the chest. Her breath caught, and for a moment, she couldn't move. The storm? The storm was a part of her? She had always believed the storm was something external, something that had threatened to consume everything around her. But now, she could feel it—the pull, the familiar weight of it. It had always been inside her. She had been the storm all along.

"No," she whispered, shaking her head, as if denying the truth would make it disappear. "No, I'm not the storm. I'm not you."

The figure stepped forward, his presence growing more powerful with each movement. "You are exactly like me, Elara. You are the Kingdom. And now you must accept it. You must embrace what you are and what you've always been. You are my chosen heir. You are the one destined to bring the Kingdom back."

Elara stumbled backward, her breath shallow, her thoughts spinning. The words were a poison, laced with truth she didn't want to hear. She had always fought the storm, fought the dark power that had consumed her world. But could it be? Could it really be that the Kingdom had never been an external force? Could it have been inside her all along?

"No," she gasped, her voice breaking. "I will never be like you."

The figure's smile widened, his eyes gleaming with an ancient malice. "You have no choice, Elara. You were born for this. The

Kingdom's blood runs through your veins. And now you will fulfill your purpose."

With that, he raised his hand, and the air around them seemed to ripple, as if the very fabric of reality was bending and warping to his will. The ground beneath Elara's feet trembled, a low, ominous rumble that grew louder with each passing second. She could feel the storm stirring within her, could feel its power rising to meet the dark force in front of her. But something inside her screamed to resist. To fight.

"No," she whispered, her voice shaking. "I won't give in. I won't be your heir."

The figure's laugh echoed through the ruins, a sound that sent a chill racing down her spine. "You already are, Elara. You've always been."

In that moment, the storm exploded within her—a wave of raw, untamed power that surged through her veins, filling her with an overwhelming sense of strength and terror. The wind picked up around her, whipping the broken remnants of the castle into a frenzy, tearing at her clothes and hair. The ground beneath her cracked, splintering like the very bones of the earth breaking free.

"Elara," the figure said, his voice rising above the chaos. "Embrace it. Embrace the storm."

She could feel the storm's power now, pulsing inside her, like an ancient force trying to take control. The winds howled around her, the sky darkening once again. But this time, she knew. She understood.

It was her choice.

She could embrace the storm, could allow it to consume her, to become the very force she had been fighting against. Or she could fight. Fight with every last ounce of strength in her.

Her heart pounded in her chest as the storm raged within her. She could feel the storm's energy—the chaos, the power, the destruction. It was all there, like a sleeping beast waiting to be unleashed.

But Elara's resolve hardened. She wasn't going to let the storm control her. She wasn't going to let him control her.

With a fierce cry, she raised the dagger high, channeling every ounce of her strength into it. The storm within her surged, and the world around her seemed to warp and twist. The figure before her moved, his eyes narrowing, his hands raised in a gesture of command.

But it was too late.

The storm she had fought for so long—to control, to contain—was now hers to wield. And with a single, decisive movement, she thrust the dagger forward, unleashing the full force of the storm.

The figure's scream echoed through the air as the energy

collided, the storm tearing through the ruins, shattering everything in its path. The sky above roiled, the ground beneath them shook violently, and for a moment, everything was pure, unrelenting chaos.

And then... silence.

When Elara opened her eyes, the storm had dissipated. The air was still, and the ruins of the castle lay in pieces around her. She looked down at the dagger in her hand, now glowing with a faint, almost imperceptible light.

The storm was gone. The Kingdom was gone. And Elara... Elara was free.

But in the distance, there was still a whisper—a faint, lingering echo that she could not shake. The storm might have been defeated, but the battle? The battle was never truly over.

28

The Weight of Silence

The ground was still trembling beneath Elara's feet as she stood amidst the ruins of the castle, the dagger in her hand still pulsing with an unnatural energy. Her breath came in ragged gasps, and her eyes darted around, scanning the broken landscape for any sign of movement. The storm had dissipated, but something lingered in the air—a quiet, unsettling presence, like the aftermath of a storm that had left too much destruction in its wake.

She turned slowly, her eyes searching the distance for the figure—the man who had been the storm, the one who had claimed the Kingdom as his own. But there was nothing. The broken walls of the castle stretched out before her, their jagged edges silhouetted against the bruised sky, but there was no sign of him. No sign of the darkness that had consumed everything she held dear.

She had won. She had shattered the Kingdom, destroyed the storm. And yet... the silence was deafening.

Elara let out a shaky breath, her hands trembling as she lowered the dagger to her side. She had been prepared for a battle—had been ready for the moment when the storm's fury would reach its peak. But now, as the air settled into an eerie stillness, she felt the weight of what had just transpired press down on her. The storm had been a force of nature, a chaos that had threatened to swallow everything, and she had fought it, defeated it. But in doing so, she had lost so much.

The lives that had been taken. The people who had fallen. The kingdom that had crumbled into dust. All of it was a sacrifice. A price paid for freedom.

And yet, as she looked around, she couldn't shake the feeling that the price was not yet paid in full. There was something else. Something waiting.

"Elara," Daniel's voice broke through her thoughts, low and strained. She hadn't even realized he was standing behind her, his hand resting on the hilt of his sword as if ready for another fight, even though there was no longer an enemy to face. "Is it over?"

His question hung in the air, heavy with doubt. Elara turned toward him, meeting his gaze. His face was pale, his eyes wide with uncertainty. He had stood by her through every battle, every moment of doubt, and yet now, even he seemed unsure of what had come next.

"I don't know," she said quietly, her voice distant. She was still shaken, still reeling from the storm's fury that had coursed through her veins only moments before. "I think it's over, but... I'm not sure."

Daniel's brows furrowed in concern, but he didn't press her. He stepped closer, his gaze flickering between her and the ruins that surrounded them. "The storm's gone. The castle's destroyed. The Kingdom is..." He trailed off, as if searching for the right words. "It's all gone, Elara."

Elara swallowed hard, her chest tight. "I don't know. I don't think we can ever be certain it's truly gone. The Kingdom... it was never just about the storm. It was about the people, the blood, the history that's buried in this land. It was built on lies, on power, on control." Her voice broke slightly, and she closed her eyes for a moment, forcing herself to steady her breath. "And no matter how much we fight, we can't erase that so easily."

Daniel said nothing, but Elara could feel his gaze on her, a silent understanding between them. He knew what she was feeling. He knew that this victory, if it could be called that, was not as sweet as she had imagined it would be.

The wind whispered through the broken arches of the castle, a quiet, mournful sound that seemed to reflect the sorrow in her heart. Elara glanced at the horizon again, her eyes narrowing as a flicker of movement caught her attention.

Something was there.

A figure.

It wasn't the storm. It wasn't the shadow of the man who had haunted her dreams. But it was something. Someone. Someone walking slowly across the field of ruins, their form moving with a calm, almost deliberate pace.

Elara's breath caught in her throat. Her instincts flared, and without thinking, she moved forward, the dagger still in her hand, ready for whatever threat might approach. But as she stepped into the open, the figure stopped.

And she recognized them.

"Ronan?" she called out, her voice a mixture of confusion and disbelief.

The figure didn't respond, but Elara knew it was him. Ronan—the man who had once been her closest ally, who had fought beside her against the storm, against the Kingdom. The same man who had disappeared without a trace, leaving her to fight alone.

"Ronan!" she called again, more urgently this time.

He stopped walking, his back to her as if unsure whether to acknowledge her presence. His broad shoulders were slumped slightly, his once-pristine armor battered and worn, as if he had seen the ravages of war firsthand. But there was something else in his posture—a heaviness that didn't belong.

He turned slowly, his face shadowed beneath the hood of his cloak. Elara couldn't read his expression, but she could see the faintest hint of something in his eyes—something that made her chest tighten with dread.

"You shouldn't have come back," he said, his voice flat, devoid of the warmth it had once held.

"Ronan, what—what happened to you?" Elara's voice trembled as she took a step toward him, trying to bridge the distance between them. "We thought you were dead. I thought you were—"

"I'm not dead, Elara," he interrupted, his tone sharp. "But I wish I were."

Her heart sank at his words. "What are you talking about?" she asked, her voice barely a whisper. "You don't mean that."

Ronan's eyes flickered toward the ground, and for a moment, Elara saw a flash of something—regret, guilt, pain. But it was gone before she could grasp it. He seemed distant, as though he were seeing something far beyond her.

"You don't understand," he said softly, his voice breaking. "You never could. I... I was the one who helped bring the storm to the Kingdom. I didn't know, not at first. But I helped the forces that bound it to this world. And now..." His voice trailed off, as if the weight of what he was confessing was too much to bear. "Now it's here again, Elara. The storm didn't die. It just... changed."

Elara's pulse quickened, and her hand instinctively tightened around the dagger. "What are you saying?"

"I'm saying that I didn't just betray the Kingdom. I betrayed you, Elara. I let the storm grow, and I thought I could control it. But now..." He lifted his eyes to meet hers, and she saw the flicker of hopelessness in them. "It's not over. Not for me. Not for any of us."

The weight of his words hit her like a punch to the gut. "You're telling me that the storm..." Her voice cracked as she forced herself to ask the question. "It's still here?"

Ronan nodded, his face grim. "It was never truly gone. It was always inside me. Inside all of us who believed in the Kingdom. And now, it's come back. Stronger than ever."

Elara felt the ground beneath her feet shift, the silence around them growing heavier. The storm hadn't just been an external force—it had been inside them, woven into the very fabric of their beings. And now it had returned, waiting for the right moment to strike again.

"I thought I could control it," Ronan whispered, as though speaking to himself. "But I was wrong. The storm controls us."

Elara's mind raced. If the storm hadn't truly been destroyed, if it was still inside Ronan—and perhaps inside others—then how could she ever truly be free?

"How do we stop it?" she demanded, her voice sharp, desperate. "How do we stop it, Ronan?"

But Ronan's eyes were distant, as though he had already accepted the truth.

"We don't," he said softly. "We never could."

The weight of his words pressed down on Elara, and the dagger in her hand felt like a stone. There was no victory. No end to this.

The storm had come back.

And it would never leave.

29

The Echo of Shadows

Elara stood motionless, her eyes locked on Ronan, her body trembling as the weight of his words settled deep within her chest. The wind stirred the remnants of the castle, sending shards of stone and broken wood drifting through the air. The world felt hollow now, like an echo bouncing between the fractured walls of a place long lost.

"Ronan, you—" Her voice faltered. She couldn't finish the thought. How could she? How could she process the fact that everything they had fought for had been for nothing?

He turned away from her, his face buried beneath the shadow of his hood. His steps were slow, deliberate, as if he had already given up on whatever hope remained in the world. Elara's heart pounded in her chest, and she took a step forward, reaching out to him, though her hand trembled at the thought of touching him again.

"Ronan!" she called, her voice rising with desperation. "Please, tell me how to stop it. There has to be a way."

He paused, his shoulders sagging as if the mere weight of her words were too much to carry. Slowly, he turned to face her, his eyes heavy with sorrow. They no longer held the fire she had once admired, the fire that had driven him to fight beside her. They were dull now, filled with a quiet resignation.

"There is no stopping it," he whispered. "You should know that by now. We are all bound to it. The storm—it's not just a force of nature. It's a curse. A curse that was woven into the very foundation of this Kingdom, and you, Elara, you're the last piece of it."

Elara recoiled as though struck. The dagger in her hand felt suddenly cold and foreign, a weapon she didn't know how to wield anymore. A weapon that had once symbolized her hope, now nothing more than a cruel reminder of what she had lost. She had thought that by defeating the storm, by shattering the Kingdom's throne, she would free herself from the weight of the curse. But instead, she had only sealed her fate.

"No," she breathed, shaking her head. "I didn't—"

"You didn't think it would be this way, did you?" Ronan's voice was sharp now, tinged with something that might have been bitterness, or perhaps despair. "You thought you could break the chains, free the people, destroy the Kingdom and the storm would fade into nothingness. But the storm is not a thing to be destroyed. It is a part of us. It has always been a part of us."

Elara's thoughts swirled in confusion, her mind struggling to grasp the enormity of what Ronan was saying. "But you—" she began, her words stumbling over each other, "you were a part of the Kingdom too. You were supposed to help me."

"I did," Ronan interrupted, his gaze hardening, as if the very idea of her questioning him was an affront. "I helped you because I believed we could rid ourselves of the storm. I believed we could take the Kingdom back. But the truth is, Elara, there was no escape from it. Not for you, not for me, and not for anyone who ever touched this land."

The silence that followed felt suffocating, the air thick with unspoken truths. Elara's chest tightened, her breath shallow as she tried to comprehend the weight of Ronan's admission. She had trusted him. She had believed in him—just as she had believed in herself. And now, everything she had known was slipping through her fingers like sand.

"You're lying," she finally said, her voice trembling with anger and disbelief. "You're telling me this just to make me give up."

Ronan's expression remained unreadable, but there was something in his eyes—something that told her he wasn't lying. That the storm, the curse, was far more than anything they could have anticipated.

The ground beneath their feet seemed to shift then, as if the earth itself was stirring with the same restless energy that had plagued the Kingdom for so long. The wind howled, sharp and cold, whipping through the ruins of the castle and sending a chill through Elara's bones. She felt it—the pulse of something dark, something ancient, awakening beneath the surface. The storm was not gone. It had never been gone.

"It's not just a storm," Ronan continued, his voice growing more distant. "It's a force that has shaped everything in this Kingdom. It feeds on fear, on ambition, on the desire for power. It has taken root in every soul that has ever lived here. And now that the Kingdom is shattered, now that the power has crumbled, the storm will find a new vessel."

Elara's stomach turned. "You mean... me."

Ronan nodded grimly. "Yes. The storm was always meant for you. You were always meant to carry it."

"No," Elara gasped, stepping back as though the very air between them had grown toxic. "No, I won't let it—"

"You don't have a choice," he said flatly. "You've already taken the dagger, haven't you? You've already bound yourself to it."

The dagger. She had thought she had chosen it out of necessity—out of hope. But now, she realized that it had chosen her long before she ever understood its true power. The storm had been inside her from the moment she held it. It had been waiting, waiting for the right time to awaken.

The ground rumbled again, and Elara stumbled as the castle trembled underfoot. She looked around, her mind racing. Was it the storm? Had it grown too powerful to contain, too desperate to remain silent? Or was it something else?

"Ronan," she said, forcing herself to steady her breath, "how do I stop it? If it's in me, then how do I rid myself of it?"

"You can't," he said softly, shaking his head. "The only way to rid yourself of the storm is to embrace it."

Elara felt the words sink in like cold steel. "Embrace it?" she whispered, her voice thick with disbelief. "How do you expect me to do that? To become a part of the storm?"

"You already are," Ronan said, his voice empty, hollow. "The storm lives inside of you, Elara. It is your shadow, your reflection. It has shaped everything you are—your strength, your will, your heart. You can't defeat it. You can't escape it. You can only join it."

The castle groaned again, louder this time, and Elara felt the ground shift beneath her feet. Her heart hammered in her chest as she took another step backward, her mind swimming with the horror of Ronan's words. Was there truly no way out? Was she doomed to carry this storm, this darkness, for the rest of her life?

"How do I join it?" she asked, her voice barely a whisper, barely a plea.

Ronan's face softened for a moment, as if he were truly grieving for what was about to happen. "There is no choice, Elara. It's not about fighting anymore. It's about accepting your fate.

The storm will never be gone. It will always return, stronger, darker, until it consumes everything. It consumes us all."

For the first time, Elara allowed herself to truly look at him—to see the man who had been her friend, her confidante, and now, the harbinger of this terrible truth. His face was a mask of regret and sorrow, but there was nothing left for him to offer her.

"You have to let it take you," he said, his voice soft. "You have to let the storm in, Elara. Only then can you free everyone else."

The words hung in the air, suffocating her. She wanted to scream, to deny it, to fight against the inevitable. But deep down, she knew the truth. She had always known. There was no way to fight the storm. Not now. Not ever.

And as the castle trembled again, Elara felt the pull of the darkness growing stronger. The storm had found its vessel.

It was her.

And there was no turning back.

30

The Heart of the Storm

Elara's heart thundered in her chest as she stood on the shattered grounds of the castle, the winds rising around her, stirring the remnants of the fallen Kingdom. The weight of Ronan's words still clung to her, suffocating, oppressive. The storm was inside her. It had always been inside her. She could feel it now, deep in her bones, like a dark tide rising within, thrashing to be freed. And yet, a small, defiant spark within her refused to surrender.

Ronan's figure loomed in the distance, his eyes hollow with the knowledge of what he had done to her, and what had been done to the Kingdom. Elara wanted to call out to him, to demand answers, to make him understand the choice she had not made—no, the choice she refused to make. But the words caught in her throat, and a strange, crushing silence pressed in on her.

"You have to embrace it," Ronan's voice echoed, his words like an iron chain pulling her deeper into the storm's grasp. "There is no escape. The storm is you. It always has been."

The castle groaned around her, as though the stone itself was remembering the fury it had once weathered. Elara turned, her eyes searching the ruins for some sign of the man who had bound the storm to the Kingdom. The one who had set this twisted fate in motion. But there was no sign of him now. No indication that anything—anything at all—could have prevented the chaos that had unfolded.

"Elara."

The voice came from behind her, soft, familiar, and so full of pain that it made her stomach lurch. She didn't need to turn to know who it was. She knew that voice. She would recognize it anywhere.

She spun around, and there he was—Daniel. His face was grim, his dark eyes heavy with sorrow. His once-immaculate armor was scratched and battered, his cloak torn. His hair was disheveled, but it was the haunted expression in his eyes that made her breath catch.

"Elara," he repeated, taking a tentative step toward her. "I don't know what's happening to you, but you have to stop. This... this isn't you. You can't let it consume you."

She opened her mouth to respond, to explain everything, but the words didn't come. Instead, she felt something within her stirring—something sharp, cold, and powerful. The storm. She could feel it pushing against her ribs, clawing to be released. It was so close, so tantalizingly close, that she could almost taste it.

"I—I don't have a choice," she finally whispered, her voice hoarse. "The storm... It's in me now. I can't fight it, Daniel. It's too strong."

"No," he said, shaking his head, his voice filled with determination. "You can fight it. You can control it. You are not a prisoner to it, Elara. You never were."

His words were like a lifeline, a flicker of light in the overwhelming darkness that threatened to swallow her whole. But they felt distant, too distant to reach. The storm pulsed inside her, a living thing, its presence undeniable and suffocating.

"I'm sorry," Elara whispered, tears filling her eyes as the storm raged within her, threatening to tear her apart. "I don't know if I can stop it. I don't know if I want to anymore."

"Don't say that," Daniel said, his voice suddenly fierce, desperate. "You're stronger than this. You always have been. Don't let it win, Elara. Don't let the storm take you."

But it wasn't his words that reached her. It was the storm. The call of the dark force that had been whispering to her since the moment she had first taken up the dagger. She could feel it now, its insistent thrum vibrating through her every cell, urging her to release it, to let it flow through her and take control.

"Elara," Daniel's voice trembled, reaching her again, but this time, there was something in his eyes—a flicker of understanding, of fear. "Please. Please don't let it take you from me."

His words pierced her like a dagger of their own. How could she explain the truth to him? That the storm was already taking her? That it had been taking her from him long before either of them had realized? That the man she had once been—the woman who had fought so hard for freedom, for peace—was slipping away, drowning in the darkness?

She stepped back, her breath shallow, the storm's pull growing stronger by the second. She could feel the edge of something terrible, something irrevocable, tugging at her heart. Her hand tightened around the dagger, the familiar weight of it offering no comfort, only a reminder of the bond she had made, the choice she had unknowingly accepted. It was hers now. And there was no escaping it.

"I have to," she said, the words trembling on her lips. "I have to let it in, Daniel."

"No," he whispered, shaking his head, stepping toward her. "You don't."

But before he could reach her, the ground beneath them rumbled, a deep, guttural growl that seemed to come from the heart of the earth itself. The sky above darkened, the wind picking up, swirling around them like a tornado. Elara's body went rigid as a voice echoed in her mind—cold, harsh, and familiar.

You cannot escape me. Not now. Not ever.

The storm, in all its terrible majesty, was calling to her. The earth groaned, the sky crackling with energy. Elara gasped as the world around her seemed to distort, the very fabric of reality bending, warping under the pressure of the storm's power. The air tasted metallic, like the sharp tang of lightning just before it struck.

"Run!" Daniel shouted, his face twisted in fear as he grabbed her arm, pulling her toward him. But Elara didn't move. She couldn't. The storm was here, inside her, and it wasn't leaving.

"Daniel," she said, her voice low and unrecognizable, the words almost lost beneath the howling winds. "I'm sorry."

She pulled away from him, stepping back into the center of the ruined courtyard. She raised the dagger, its edge gleaming in the shifting light. Her eyes closed as she let the storm flood her senses, the raw, unbridled power rushing through her veins like fire and ice. She felt it—every crack, every pulse, every moment of its fury.

Join me, the storm whispered, its voice a thousand voices, each one darker than the last. Embrace what you are, Elara. We are one.

She felt it then—the storm, not as an enemy, but as a part of her, entwined in her very soul. It was as though the veil between her and the darkness had lifted, and she understood at last. She had always been the storm. She had always been the one it sought.

Her heart beat faster as she allowed herself to feel it, to let the storm into her without resistance. Power surged through her, raw and terrifying. She was no longer a victim. She was the storm.

"No!" Daniel shouted, rushing toward her, but the wind knocked him back, throwing him to the ground as though the very air was fighting him. Elara's eyes snapped open, and for the first time, she saw what she had become. What she had always been.

She raised her hands to the sky, her breath coming in ragged gasps as the storm above her coiled and writhed like a living thing. The world around them seemed to tremble, the ground cracking open beneath their feet, the air alive with the force of the storm.

It is not over, the storm's voice whispered again, and Elara let out a low, guttural laugh. It will never be over.

The wind howled, the sky split open with thunder, and for a moment, Elara stood at the heart of it all, her body pulsing with the power of the storm. The world around her was unraveling. And yet, in that moment, she felt whole.

The storm had found its queen.

And she had no intention of letting it go.

31

The Appraisal

The wind howled through the broken windows of the castle, carrying with it the smell of rain, earth, and decay. Elara stood in the center of the great hall, the dim light of the dying flames flickering across the cold stone walls. The storm outside was louder than it had ever been, a furious, unrelenting force that seemed to echo the chaos within her. Her breath came in shallow, rapid gasps as she tried to steady herself, but the energy, the power that had once felt like a blessing now consumed her. The weight of it pressed down on her chest, suffocating her.

She could feel it—feel the storm tightening its grip around her heart, around her mind. The connection, the bond she had once welcomed, was now something darker, something far more dangerous than she had ever imagined. She could hear it, a constant whisper beneath the thunder, calling her name, pulling her toward the inevitable. *You are mine*, it seemed to say. *There is no escaping me.*

The door creaked open behind her, and Elara spun around, her heart leaping into her throat. She had no idea how long she had been standing there, alone in the shadows, but she knew that whoever had come now had not come to bring comfort.

"Daniel..." she breathed, her voice raw, as though she hadn't spoken in days. The name felt strange on her tongue, like a memory that didn't belong to her anymore.

He stepped forward, his eyes dark with concern and something else—something that Elara couldn't quite place. He didn't speak at first. Instead, he just watched her, as though searching for something in her face, something she couldn't hide. But there was no hiding it now. Not anymore.

"You've been avoiding me," Daniel said quietly, his tone strained, as though the words themselves were too heavy for him to carry. He had always been the one to shield her, to protect her from the storm. But now, there was no shielding. Not from the storm, not from herself.

"I didn't know how to face you," Elara replied, her voice breaking. She couldn't meet his eyes. She couldn't face the man who had once been her anchor when everything else had crumbled around her. How could she? She was no longer the same woman who had leaned on him for strength. The storm had changed her in ways she couldn't explain, and she feared that if she let him see what she had become, it would destroy him too.

Daniel's expression softened, but only for a moment. He closed the distance between them, his steps slow, deliberate. "Elara," he said, his voice low but firm, "this isn't you. You don't have to do this. You don't have to let it consume you."

The storm raged outside, and for a moment, Elara thought she could hear it in his voice, too—there was something wild, something desperate beneath his calm exterior. He was afraid. Not of the storm, but of what it had done to her. Of what she was becoming.

But Elara couldn't stop. She couldn't pretend like she wasn't feeling it—the storm's pull, its hunger. Every passing moment, it sank deeper into her, clawing at her insides. She had thought she could fight it, but now, with Daniel standing before her, she realized something terrifying: *She didn't want to fight it anymore.*

"Elara, look at me," Daniel demanded, his voice rising with a sense of urgency she hadn't heard before. "You're not alone in this. We can fix this, together."

She raised her eyes to meet his, and what she saw there took her breath away. His gaze wasn't just full of concern—it was filled with a kind of helplessness that she hadn't expected, that she didn't know how to deal with. It was the same look that had crossed her face when she realized that she was losing control, when the storm had started to unravel her from the inside out.

"I don't know how to fix it," Elara whispered, tears brimming in her eyes. "I don't know how to go back."

"You don't need to go back," Daniel said, his hand gently reaching for hers. The warmth of his touch was familiar, a tether to the past, a lifeline she so desperately needed. But even as she grasped his hand, she felt the storm surge within her, a wild force that made her pull away. "You just need to stay here. With me."

The silence between them grew heavy, and the storm outside seemed to roar louder in the stillness. Elara felt a pang of longing, a desperate yearning for the life they had shared before everything had changed. She wanted to believe him. She wanted to believe that this was just a phase, that somehow, she could return to the woman she once was. But she knew better now. She knew that the storm was not just something external—it was inside her. And the more she resisted it, the more it claimed her.

"You don't understand," Elara said, shaking her head, the words coming out in a tortured sob. "I can feel it, Daniel. The storm—it's inside me. And I can't fight it anymore. It's too strong. I don't even know if I *want* to fight it."

Daniel's face fell, and for the first time, Elara saw fear in his eyes. Fear not of the storm, but of what she was becoming. "You don't mean that," he said, his voice breaking. "You can't mean that."

But Elara only stared at him, her chest tightening, the storm growing louder, stronger with every breath she took. She could feel its presence now, swirling inside her, like a living thing, clawing its way deeper into her soul.

"I'm sorry, Daniel," she said, her voice barely a whisper. "I don't know who I am anymore."

The words hit him like a physical blow, and for a moment, he just stood there, his face pale and drawn. The air between them was thick with unspoken things—things neither of them wanted to say, but both of them feared were true. The storm had torn them apart, and there was no fixing it. No going back.

"Elara," Daniel said softly, his voice full of pain, "I'm not going to give up on you. Not now. Not ever."

But his words didn't reach her. Not anymore. She could feel the storm inside her, louder now, almost suffocating. It was growing stronger, taking over, and she didn't know how much longer she could keep up the facade. The storm was inside her. It had always been inside her. And it was calling her home.

"Elara, please," Daniel pleaded, his voice desperate, "you have to fight this. I need you to fight. We can't lose you."

But Elara had already made her choice. The storm was her

destiny now, and she had no power to deny it any longer. She could feel it wrapping around her heart, seeping into her bones, taking her in. And as much as it terrified her, she knew deep down that it was too late to turn back.

With one last glance at Daniel, Elara turned away. She could hear him calling after her, but she didn't stop. She couldn't. There was no turning back now.

She stepped toward the open doors of the great hall, her heart heavy with the weight of what she was about to do. The storm was waiting for her. The storm had always been waiting for her.

And as the doors swung open, the wind howled through the hall, a welcome and a warning.

Elara closed her eyes, and stepped into the storm.

32

A Flicker in the Dark

The darkness stretched before her, a suffocating void that seemed to swallow everything in its path. Elara stood at the edge of it, her heart pounding, her body trembling from the forces swirling within and around her. The storm raged on, its fury a constant hum in her ears, as though it were alive—watching her, waiting for her to make the next move.

For weeks now, she had felt its presence, that insistent pulse of darkness that had slowly consumed every part of her being. The storm had taken root in her soul, woven itself into the very fabric of her thoughts, her fears, and her desires. It was her, and she was it. There was no separating them anymore.

But now, standing on the precipice of something far darker than she had ever imagined, Elara felt the faintest flicker of something else—a glimmer of hope buried deep within the abyss.

She took a shallow breath, her fingers curling around the

dagger in her hand, the cold metal pressing against her palm like an old, familiar friend. She could feel its power, its connection to the storm. The dagger had been the key, the instrument that had bound her to the darkness in the first place. But now, it felt different. The storm was no longer the same, and neither was she.

The winds howled louder, and Elara's eyes narrowed as she scanned the horizon. She had come here, to this forsaken place, to confront the truth. To face the consequences of the choices she had made. But what if the truth was more than she could bear? What if the storm was far more powerful than even she had come to realize?

The castle ruins behind her loomed like silent sentinels, their broken walls standing as a testament to the destruction the storm had wrought. There was nothing left here—no life, no hope, just the ruins of a Kingdom that had once been filled with dreams of peace and power. All of it had been reduced to ashes, and now, only the storm remained.

"Elara."

The voice was low, barely a whisper against the howling wind. Yet, Elara knew it. She had heard it before. She spun around, her breath catching in her throat as she saw him standing there—Ronan.

He looked different, his face gaunt, his eyes shadowed with a sorrow that seemed to consume him. His clothes were tattered, his once-pristine cloak now nothing more than torn rags. But it wasn't his appearance that sent a chill through Elara's veins. It was the look in his eyes. The same look that had haunted her since the day they had first crossed paths.

"Ronan," she breathed, her voice a mixture of disbelief and relief. "You're alive."

He nodded, but there was no joy in the motion. Only a deep, profound sadness that made Elara's heart ache. "Alive, yes. But not as I once was."

She took a hesitant step toward him, her mind racing with questions. "What do you mean? What happened? I thought you were—"

"I know," he interrupted, his voice barely audible over the wind. "You thought I was gone. You thought you had won." His eyes hardened as he looked at her, his expression turning colder. "But you don't understand, Elara. This... this isn't over."

Her stomach twisted as his words settled in, a feeling of dread creeping up her spine. "What are you talking about?"

"You've become the storm," Ronan said, his tone flat, devoid of any warmth. "The curse is inside of you, and there is no escaping it. The Kingdom is gone, yes. But the storm... it will always find a way to return. It always has."

Elara shook her head, her grip tightening on the dagger. "No. I... I can stop it. I have to stop it."

"You can't," Ronan said, his voice cold and distant. "You've already become one with it. You've embraced it, Elara. There's no turning back now."

For a moment, the world around them seemed to still, the howling wind fading into a deafening silence. Elara's pulse raced, her breath coming in shallow gasps. She had been warned. By Ronan. By the storm itself. And yet, she had clung to the hope that she could somehow, somehow break free from its grip.

But deep down, she knew. She knew that she had already crossed the line. That the storm was not just something outside of her—it was within her. It had always been within her.

"No," she whispered, the words tasting bitter on her tongue. "I won't let it take me. I won't be its puppet. I will find a way."

Ronan's gaze softened for a fleeting moment, as if he were trying to find some shred of the woman he had once known, but it was quickly replaced by the same hardened resolve. "You're already too far gone."

"I am not," she shot back, her voice rising with defiance. "I am not like you."

Ronan flinched at her words, his expression darkening as he took a step back. "You think I wanted this? You think I wanted to become the thing I feared most?"

Elara's breath caught in her throat as a terrible realization sank in. She had seen it in his eyes, felt it in his words, but it wasn't until now that she truly understood the depth of his despair.

"You... you've already embraced it," she whispered, her voice trembling. "Haven't you?"

He didn't answer immediately, and in that silence, Elara knew the truth. Ronan had given in. He had accepted the storm as part of him, just as she had been forced to. He had surrendered to the darkness long before her.

"I didn't have a choice," he said finally, his voice hollow. "None of us do. The storm isn't something you can control. It's not something you can escape. It's a part of this Kingdom, and it always will be. You're the last of us, Elara. The last piece of the puzzle."

Elara's mind raced, her heart hammering in her chest as she looked at him, her hands shaking. The storm, the curse—it wasn't just a weapon. It wasn't just a force of nature. It was a curse that had been woven into the very soul of the Kingdom. And now, it was hers to bear.

"No," she whispered again, the denial more desperate this time. "I won't be like you. I won't let it consume me."

But even as she spoke, the winds began to pick up again, swirling around them in a violent, furious crescendo. Elara staggered back, the storm's power rising with every heartbeat, its energy crackling through the air like a thousand live wires.

"You're already too late," Ronan said softly, almost pityingly. "The storm knows you. It knows your fears, your weaknesses. And it will make you bow to it."

"No," Elara cried, her voice raw with anguish. "I won't give in. I won't let it destroy me."

And then, with a cry that pierced the air, she raised the dagger high above her head, its blade gleaming in the light of the storm. She felt the storm's power crackling through her veins, urging her to strike, to end it all. But this time, something inside her resisted. A flicker of something else—a flicker of her old self, the one who had fought against the darkness, who had believed in the possibility of light.

For a brief moment, the winds stilled, the air around her hanging heavy with tension. She felt the storm's presence, felt it pushing against her, urging her to give in. But Elara stood firm, her grip on the dagger unwavering.

"No," she whispered again, but this time, it wasn't a denial. It was a promise.

The storm was not going to take her. Not today. Not ever.

With a sudden, defiant movement, she plunged the dagger into the ground. The earth trembled beneath her, and the storm seemed to roar in fury, its power surging around her like a tidal wave.

But Elara stood tall, her heart steady, her soul defiant. She had made her choice.

And for the first time in a long time, she felt the flicker of hope.

33

The Breaking Point

The earth trembled beneath Elara's feet, its vibrations pulsing through her bones, as though the very land itself were alive with fury. The storm had become a living, breathing entity, and she was the eye of it. It swirled around her, a dark, violent mass of wind and rain that seemed to crackle with ancient power. It was as though the very forces of nature were battling within her, and the world itself was waiting for her to decide which side would win.

The dagger that had once been an instrument of her doom now felt strangely weightless in her grip. Its blade shimmered with an eerie light, a constant reminder of the pact she had made, the storm that had bound itself to her. But there was no comfort in its familiarity anymore. Instead, it felt like a chain, holding her in place, refusing to let her move.

"Elara."

The voice was distant at first, carried by the wind, and yet it cut through the storm like a blade. Elara's heart skipped a beat as she turned toward the sound. She knew that voice. She had heard it in her dreams, in her nightmares, and in the echoes of her memory.

It was Daniel.

Her heart ached at the thought of him. How long had it been since she had seen him, since she had felt his presence beside her? It felt like an eternity, like a lifetime had passed since their paths had first crossed. And yet, despite everything, despite the storm, despite the darkness that had overtaken her, she could still hear his voice in her mind, soft and steady, calling her back from the edge.

"Elara, you have to stop."

She spun around, her breath catching in her throat as she saw him standing there, his figure emerging from the darkness like a ghost. His clothes were torn, his face smeared with dirt and sweat, but his eyes were the same—the same familiar gaze that had once anchored her, that had once made her believe that there was hope.

"Daniel," she whispered, her voice breaking. "How... how did you find me?"

He stepped toward her, his expression a mixture of concern and determination. "I never stopped looking for you," he said, his voice low but filled with conviction. "You think I would just let you disappear into this storm? No, Elara. You're not alone.

You never were."

Elara's breath caught in her throat as his words hit her like a wave. You're not alone. It was a simple phrase, but in that moment, it felt like the world itself had shifted. For so long, she had carried the weight of the storm alone, convinced that there was no one left who could understand, no one who could help. But here he was, standing before her, a beacon of light in the suffocating darkness.

"Elara," Daniel said again, his voice urgent now, "you have to listen to me. This storm—it's not you. It's not who you are. You've become something else. But you don't have to stay like this. You can still fight it."

She wanted to believe him. She wanted to believe that there was a way out of this, that there was a way to break free from the storm's grip. But the truth was, she didn't know anymore. She didn't know if she could control it, if she could resist it.

"The storm is me, Daniel," she whispered, the words bitter on her tongue. "I am the storm. It's too late to stop it now."

"No," he said, his voice hardening with resolve. "It's not too late. You've always been stronger than this, Elara. You're not the storm. You never were. You're the one who can control it, not the other way around."

Her heart thudded painfully in her chest as his words sank in. Could he be right? Could she still find a way to fight the storm, to regain control over her own life?

The wind howled louder, as though in defiance, its force pushing against her, tugging at the very core of her being. The storm didn't want her to believe what Daniel had said. It didn't want her to let go of the power it had given her, the power that had become so familiar, so intoxicating.

But Daniel's words held something that the storm could not take from her. They held the memory of who she had been before the storm had consumed her. They held the promise of something more—something beyond the darkness.

She looked at him, her eyes filled with a mixture of desperation and hope. "I don't know if I can," she said, her voice trembling. "I don't know if I'm strong enough."

"You are," Daniel said firmly. "You've always been. Elara, you've been through so much. You've fought for everything you've ever wanted, and you've survived. You're not weak. You're stronger than you know."

His words stirred something deep inside her, a flicker of the woman she had once been, a woman who had stood tall in the face of adversity, who had refused to let the darkness define her. It was that woman who had once stood in the ruins of this very castle, looking at the world with hope in her heart. She had wanted to build something better. Something stronger. And she had almost done it.

Almost.

But now, the storm was all that remained. And yet... perhaps it didn't have to be that way.

"Elara," Daniel said softly, taking a step closer to her. "You're not the storm. You're the light that can stop it."

His words echoed in her mind, a lifeline that reached through the storm's darkness. Could she really be the light? Could she really be the one to end this, to undo everything that had been done?

The storm raged louder, a deafening roar that filled her ears, but for the first time, Elara felt something different—a stillness, a calm at the center of the chaos. It was like the eye of the storm, and in that moment, she realized that it wasn't too late. The storm didn't define her. She defined the storm.

With trembling hands, she raised the dagger once more, the blade gleaming in the faint light that cut through the storm. The wind howled around her, but she stood firm. She was not going to let the storm control her any longer.

For the first time in a long while, Elara felt a surge of power—not the dark, oppressive force of the storm, but something lighter, something purer. It was hope. It was strength. It was everything she had once been, everything she could still be.

"I can do this," she whispered to herself, her voice steady, her resolve solidifying. "I can end this."

Daniel watched her, his eyes filled with a mixture of relief and awe. "Elara…"

But she didn't need his encouragement anymore. The storm may have been inside her, but it didn't own her. She would never let it take her again.

With a final, defiant cry, Elara thrust the dagger into the ground. The earth trembled beneath her feet, the sky above her crackling with energy. For a moment, everything seemed to pause, as though the very world was holding its breath.

And then, with a deafening roar, the storm exploded outward, a wave of energy that seemed to shatter the air itself. The winds howled in fury, but Elara stood firm, her body alight with the power of the storm—her power. The storm that had once consumed her was now a force she could wield. A force she could control.

The storm didn't stop. It didn't fade. But it was no longer the same. It no longer controlled her.

And for the first time in a long time, Elara felt the weight of the storm lift. The darkness that had once consumed her began to recede, replaced by the flicker of light, the flicker of hope.

The breaking point had come.

And Elara had chosen to break free.

www.ingramcontent.com/pod-product-compliance
Lightning Source LLC
LaVergne TN
LVHW011935070526
838202LV00054B/4649